History, Legacy, and the Law

History, Legacy, and the Law

The Birth, Majesty, and Preservation of the United States of America

PAULINE CUSACK
With a chapter by Belinda Stanley

EAKIN PRESS Austin, Texas

In memory of my father,

Paul Robert Pearce,

who lived it.

For CIP
information,
please access:
www.loc.gov

FIRST EDITION
Copyright © 2002
By Pauline Cusack
Published in the United States of America
By Eakin Press
A Division of Sunbelt Media, Inc.
P.O. Drawer 90159 ⌁ Austin, Texas 78709-0159
email: eakinpub@sig.net
🖳 website: www.eakinpress.com 🖳
ALL RIGHTS RESERVED.
1 2 3 4 5 6 7 8 9
1-57168-655-X PB
1-57186-604-5 HB

Contents

Acknowledgments / v

Preface / 1

Chapter One / 5
Natural Law, The Ancients, and the Word

Chapter Two / 12
Natural Law, Family, and Society

Chapter Three / 16
The Birth of Christ and the Rebirth of Man

Chapter Four / 21
The Puritan Quest for Freedom

Chapter Five / 32
The Spirit of the Revolution and Constitution

Chapter Six / 43
Intellectual Elitism, Gnosticism, and the Great Lie

Chapter Seven / 56
Education, Socialism, and Secular Humanism

Chapter Eight / 74
The Responsibilities of Citizenship

Chapter Nine / 82
When Government Does Too Much

Chapter Ten / 90
Special Interests: An Excess of Power

Chapter Eleven / 93
Taxes: Socialism and Plunder

Chapter Twelve / 99
Economics and the Battle for Freedom

Chapter Thirteen / 112
Equality, Perception, and Faith

Chapter Fourteen / 118
Marriage: A Pact With God

Chapter Fifteen / 128
Abortion: Human By Degrees?

Chapter Sixteen / 133
Rational Environmentalism

Chapter Seventeen / 141
Animal Rights: Equality, or Stewardship?

Chapter Eighteen / 149
The Ripple In the Pond

Epilogue / 157

Endnotes / 159

Bibliography / 165

Index / 169

About the Author / 175

Acknowledgments

I owe a great debt that can never be fully repaid to Joan Puryear. She typed the manuscript from the original handwritten work. Her patience and endurance cannot be overstated. Her faith in my project sustained me throughout. The chapter on environment was written by Belinda Stanley. I deeply appreciate her commitment in an area where I felt my scientific expertise was lacking. There have been so many wonderful people, among them The Reverend Mr. Edmund A. Opitz, whose correspondence pointed the way, and Dr. F. W. Mattox of Harding College, whom I thank for his generosity in permitting me use of some of his lecture notes and diagrams. The work of Verna Hall and the Foundation for Christian Education in the compilation of the material and documents included in the two volumes, *The Christian History of the Constitution of the United States of America, Christian Self-Government* and *The Christian History of the Constitution of the United States of America, Christian Self-Government with Union* was invaluable. Thank you to Tommy LeFan, who checked biblical references, and Martha Kingston, who made so many copies. A special note of thanks to Angela Buckley, who has gone through the final steps with me to bring this book to publication. Lastly to my husband, Michael, who always encourages me in all my endeavors, thank you for being there.

Preface

I have endeavored to weave history with the legacy of the founding fathers who sought God's divine guidance in framing our Constitution, and to examine moral and civil law as they apply to our society at present.

One doesn't have to search very long to find examples of anger, wrath, frustration, and indignation in the United States today. Most of us suffer the effects of these problems every day and feel helpless to alter the situation. Worse still, we blame one another, perpetuating a cycle of hatred. It is easy to overlook the fact that larger, systemic pressures are creating this problem.

Our civil and criminal justice systems are demoralized by inequity of law; regulations prevent freedom in buying, selling, and the exercise of trade and commerce; control of private property is threatened; and lastly, the government intrudes itself into our daily lives, even to point of violating our consciences.

The conscience is the voice of God inside each of us, and when we are forced by our society to disregard that voice, anger and frustration result. When manmade law, natural law, and spiritual law are in conflict, our whole society is weakened. In order to bring these different laws into balance, we must first seek to understand each of them, how they function, how they affect us.

These laws and their relationships to one another are best understood through examining history—the history of customs, beliefs, philosophies, political currents, inventions, discoveries, and persecutions. Studying history shows that manmade law has not always been independent of natural and spiritual law. The Old Testament, for instance, is a source of natural, civil, and spiritual law. When we seek to understand how these laws came into disharmony, we must endeavour to understand:

- The Greeks' acknowledgement of such powers as Nebuchadnezzar, Cyrus, Darius, and Haziel of Jehovah
- New Testament descriptions of the early church
- The corruption of the Middle Ages
- The discoveries of the Renaissance
- The perseverance of the great reformers, and
- The faith in God sustained by Christians through the great persecutions.

These and other important historical markers can lead us to uncover the causes of the helplessness and frustration we perceive today. It is a truism that those who do not study history are doomed to repeat the mistakes of the past. Just as communism and socialism didn't work in the 1600s, they didn't work in the 1900s. Maybe this time, man will study his past and not tread that path again, for it denies the individual freedom that is our birthright.

A few words about the three categories of law described in this book: spiritual law, natural law, and civil law. Each of these categories is valuable and unique. It is important, though, to be able to distinguish between them—and to bring them into proper order. Let us take the second type first: natural law. We are born free to accept or reject spiritual and civil law, but we cannot reject natural law. The law of gravity causes us to fall. If we cut ourselves, we bleed. If submerged in water too long, we drown. We all live in this world under natural law. It is a great equalizer.

People cannot reject natural law. They can reject civil law, but they will find that there are consequences for doing so. Civil law is the law of the sword to punish civil disobedience, and it is designed to protect citizens from those who have not developed self-discipline.

Spiritual law is the law of reason and persuasion, and through it we are taught our relationship to God and to our fellow man. Where all must accept natural law, and accept civil law or be punished, spiritual law may be accepted or rejected. The final result awaits us in the judgement of God. Society as a whole rejects God's law; the consequences can be seen everywhere, even though many people cannot recognize the origin of people's suffering.

Civil law is of men, but spiritual law is of the Kingdom, of which Christ is King. All powers of men, of nations, and of this world are subordinate to Him and rule by His permission and to His ultimate glory. Man tends toward greed, pride, and the quest for power; all of which are antithetical to God and Christ. In *The Reasonableness of Christianity*, philosopher John Locke describes a harmonious relationship to spiritual law:

> The Credit and Authority our Saviour and his Apostles had over the Minds of Men, by the Miracles they did, tempted them not to mix (as we find in that of all the Sects and Philosophers, and other Religions) any Conceits, any wrong Rules, any thing tending to their own By-Interest, or that of a Party, in their Morality. No Tang of Prepossession or Phansy; no Footsteps or Pride or Vanity; no Touch of Ostentation or Ambition, appears to have a hand in it.
>
> It is all pure, all sincere; nothing too much, nothing wanting; but such a compleat Rule of Life, as the wisest Men must acknowledge, tends entirely to the Good of Mankind, and that all would be happy, if all would practice it . . . .[1]

Our nation is a nation of law, predicated on the equality of mankind in the pursuit of life, liberty, and happiness. True freedom is found in the recognition of absolutes, of learning to clearly recognize right and wrong; if we know our limits and constraints, we are freed to realize our full potential without fear or terror of retribution and punishment.

James Russell Lowell, the American poet, was asked by François Guizot, a former prime minister of France, "how long the American Republic would endure?" The reply was, "As long as the principles of its founders remain dominant in the hearts of the people."[2] In another prescient moment, George Washington said in his farewell address "that the time might come in this country when some would rise seeking to undermine what they could not overthrow."

Yes, it would be difficult to overthrow our government by force, but today it is being very effectively undermined. It is this weakening of our national foundation that this book explores.

Throughout my life I have seen things in our world that I inherently knew were wrong, and I always asked myself why these things were happening. As a Christian, I had many ideas, but how could I explain them? What was reasonable? What was logical? What was true? To answer these questions, I found myself looking into history. In gaining a historical overview, I soon realized that early in this century our nation stopped making progress and began to regress. This reversal has been so insidious and so carefully concealed that it can be almost impossible to discern—especially for those of us born in the Baby Boom years and later, when the backward movement had already begun.

After the heinous attack on Pearl Harbor, December 7, 1941, Japanese admiral Yamamoto said that he feared that the only result would be that the "sleeping giant would be awakened and filled with a terrible resolve"—and it was. After the war, however, the U.S. began to put its moral values to sleep. Now that "sleeping giant" must be reawakened with a steadfast resolve to speak the truth of God, to stand firm, not to retreat, to be filled with love, peace, and humility and to hold firmly to God's teachings. We must put on the full armour of God. We are called to the arms of the spirit. Truth, righteousness, faith, salvation, "and the sword of the Spirit, which is the word of God," are our weapons, and we must wield them gently.[3]

CHAPTER ONE

Natural Law, The Ancients, and the Word

Oh, order! Material order, intellectual order, moral order! What a comfort and strength, and what an economy!
—Henri Frederic Amiel

Whether we are Christian, Muslim, Hindu, Buddhist, Jewish—even agnostic or atheist—we are all subject to natural law, for the same sun shines on us all. We have but to look around us and observe that the natural order of the universe regulates our lives and provides the model for how we should live. In our hectic society, it is easy to ignore natural order. But for the ancients, who lived in closer harmony with nature, orderliness was self-evident, and the nature of that order was considered divine. The philosopher Plato expressed appreciation for order beautifully: "God invented and gave us sight to the end that we might behold the courses of intelligence in the heaven, and apply them to the courses of our own intelligence which are akin to them ... and that we, learning them and partaking of the natural truth of reason, might imitate the absolutely unerring courses of God and regulate our own vagaries."[1]

Of course, we don't have to rely on our senses alone to perceive the orderliness of our world. Computers, given information regarding the laws of the movement of the universe, can tell us where a specific planet was or will be located at any given time, chart moon phases, and track seasonal changes. Thus modern technology confirms the orderliness of the creation. Cicero described the universal scope of this orderliness:

> True law is right reason in agreement with nature; it is of universal application, unchanging and everlasting; it summons to duty by its commands, and averts from wrong doing by its prohibitions. And it does not lay its commands or prohibitions upon good men in vain, though neither have any effect on the wicked. It is a sin to try to alter this law, nor is it allowable to attempt to repeal any part of it, and it is impossible to abolish it entirely. We cannot be freed from its obligations by senate or people, and we need not look outside ourselves for an expounder or interpreter of it. And there will not be different laws now and in the future, but one eternal and unchangeable law will be valid for all nations and all times, and there will be one master and ruler, that is; God, over us all, for he is the author of this law, its promulgator, and its enforcing judge. Whoever is disobedient is fleeing from himself and denying his human nature, and by reason of this very fact he will suffer the worst penalties, even if he escapes what is commonly considered punishment.[2]

Cicero saw that natural law came from God. William Blackstone said it this way: "This will of his Maker is called the law of nature."[3] The true beginning of the universe as we know it is revealed to man by God through the beloved apostle John: "In the beginning was the Word, and the Word was with God, and the Word was God. And the light shineth in darkness; and the darkness comprehended it not." (John 1:1-5). This is a statement of Christ's existence, his divinity, and the workmanship of creation. But, we are told, "the darkness comprehended it not"; in other words, the world did not understand.

The Creator also established the laws of motion by which the universe is protected and propelled: "Because that which may be known of God is manifest in [the heavens]; for God hath showed it unto them. For the invisible things of him from the creation of the world are clearly seen, being understood by the things that are made, even his eternal power and Godhead; so that they are without excuse" (Romans 1:19-20).

Intellectuals will have us believe that truth is relative. But nature's truths are absolute. For a scientist to claim a scientific truth, any experiment he conducts regarding a specific principle must be repeatable with the same result. If the experiment always produces the same result, it is true; if not, it is false. The movement of the universe and its bodies through space constitute our greatest laboratory for studying truth; day after day, week after week, month after month, and year after year, they adhere to the same laws, and scientific inquiries provide results that are constant, and therefore true. The reverse of this would be the absence of law, resulting in disorder and untruth. If there were no laws of operation there could be no universe. There would be nothing but chaos.

The larger question is, Where does man fit into natural law? As Plato so forcefully stated, we live in the universe and are a part of it; therefore, we are also governed by natural law.

Natural law is illustrated by the mechanics of the universe, but another important aspect of natural law is that every living thing, humans included, has its own nature. The wolf has its own nature—you may depend upon a wolf to behave in a certain way. An oak tree has its unique nature; its leaves will always be readily identifiable, true to the oak's nature. The laws of nature are fixed and unalterable for every kind of creature, plant, or mineral. The laws may be different for each, but are, in Blackstone's words, "equally fixed and invariable. The whole progress of plants, from the seed to the root, and from thence to seed again; the method of animal nutrition, digestion, secretion and all other branches of vital economy; are not left to chance or the will of the creature itself, but are performed in a wondrous involuntary manner, and guided by unerring rules laid down by the great Creator."

Blackstone further explained that these laws were to aid us in "regulating and restraining" our free will and give us "the faculty of reason to discover the purport of those laws."[4]

The word "nature" comes from the Latin *nasci*, which means "to be born." Our nature is fixed at birth. The highest creature, man, is also bound to his nature, which is to be a reasoning being. You might object that man has free will and therefore is not bound in this way. But free will pertains to the external choices we make, not to our deepest nature. To go against your own nature creates a type of civil war within, for natural order comes from within—it is not an external force or compulsion. If a man does not act in concert with his nature, he strives against himself as well as against God, as Plato points out.

Of all earthly creation, man is the only being that can reason, make order, and discern truth by virtue of his nature. As stated in Genesis, we are created in His image—that is to say, with the ability to think and reason. However, since we cannot create something from nothing and are not God, we can only be imitators of God. Because we have been formed by Him, it is only reasonable to acknowledge His superiority: "O man, who art thou that repliest against God? Shall the thing formed say to him that formed it, Why hast thou made me thus? Hath not the potter power over the clay, of the same lump to make one vessel unto honour, and another unto dishonour?" (Romans 9:20-21).

If you were to take a lump of clay and from one portion make a cup, from another, a vase, and from still another, a bowl, would not you, as the maker, be the one who determined the use of each piece? Are you not therefore superior to the cup, the vase, and the bowl? Of course you are. So it is with us: We are God's greatest creations, and because of this honor, we owe Him our loyalty.

The man who is chosen by a king to be his ambassador acts as his representative in another country. He speaks for the king and is treated accordingly. He is not the king, but rather a representative. He adheres to the king's policies and speaks on behalf of the king. Obviously, it is a great honor for the ambassador to be allowed to speak with the "king's voice." Does it not follow, then, that the ambassador has a grave responsibility to act in such a way that will not dishonor the king (and himself), and does he not owe loyalty to the king, who has trusted and honored him? As men, we are God's representatives and should honor Him. He has entrusted us with dominion over His creation.

God's creation of order, reason, and truth provided the stability, confidence, and security that we need in order to go about our daily lives. We do not fear that the sun will not rise to provide energy and sustenance to those things that provide for our survival. Because of this perfect order established by God, we have security and freedom of action.

That this order exists is self-evident, and that it is good is understood by reasoning minds who can comprehend that order is beneficial and stabilizing. Earlier, I quoted Plato regarding the "intelligence in the Heavens." Plato spoke of imitating the heavens so that we might comprehend their absolutely "unerring course" and thereby regulate our own activities. This does not by any interpretation mean that they control us. They do not; if they did, then we could not voluntarily appreciate their pattern of orderliness, reason, and truth. Rather, they are an example of the order, truth, and reason we should seek in our own lives. The NIV translation of Romans 1:20 reads, " For since the creation of the world God's invisible qualities—his eternal power and divine nature—have been clearly seen, being understood from what has been made, so that men are without excuse." Simply, His truth and order surround us constantly in what He created.

Proverbs 6:6-8 points to a worldly example of God's order: "Go to the ant, thou sluggard; consider her ways, and be wise: Which having no guide, overseer, or ruler, Provideth her meat in the summer, and gathereth her food in the harvest." God teaches us to work industriously, to save for the time of want and need, and that we can accomplish this without an overseer. This lesson could apply to the student attending to his studies and preparing for his exams as easily as it could apply to the father who should educate, feed, and clothe his family.

The book of Proverbs is full of examples comparing animal and human behavior. Birds, sheep, snakes, rock badgers (conies), locusts, lizards, lions, and other animals are all used as examples of human behavior or possibilities and remind us that the natural world provides the model on which we should base our lives.

Take Proverbs 30:27: "The locusts have no king, yet go they forth all of them by bands." This illustrates that like minded people can move forward through unity of purpose. Men and women can do the same; in fact, it is our obligation. Should it not be our duty through our acceptance of God's order and His position as Creator that we move forward in unity to serve Him and obey both His natural and revealed law?

It must be emphasized again that these two kinds of law are entertwined. They are mutually conceived, and the one confirms the other. The nature of the universe confirms the inspired Word. The

Scripture tells us how both of these realms are God's creations: "The Lord by wisdom hath founded the earth; by understanding hath he established the heavens. By his knowledge the depths are broken up, and the clouds drop down the dew" (Proverbs 3:19-20). And in Proverbs 8:14-17 we are reminded that man's law is an extension of God's law: "Counsel is mine, and sound wisdom: I am understanding; I have strength. By me kings reign, and princes decree justice. By me princes rule, and nobles, even all the judges of the earth. I love them that love me; and those that seek me early shall find me."

As we have seen, there are two sources of studies about natural law, the philosophers of old and the Scriptures. Plato wrote four hundred years before Christ, so by no stretch of the imagination could he have been a believer in the Mosaic Law. Therefore, what he knew to be true was revealed by the things of the universe, animate and inanimate. Another Greek philosopher, Aristotle, recognized this principle, for he wrote in his *Politics,* book VII, "For law is order, and good law is good order; but a very great multitude cannot be orderly: to introduce order into the unlimited is the work of a divine power—of such a power as holds together the universe." Without knowing the Creator, Aristotle recognized His handiwork and, most importantly, recognized the necessity of Him in order to secure "good law," which is "good order."

The writings of these ancient philosophers attest to the self-evident Godhead; these philosophies come from a world that knew Him not, but held Him in respect despite lack of knowledge of His Word. It is a great tribute. When Paul the Apostle visited Athens, he commended its citizens for their religious piety, as evidenced by their altar to the "unknown God." Paul in his speech on Mars Hill revealed to them the unknown God they had worshipped despite their ignorance.[5]

God first dealt directly with the patriarchs Adam, Enoch, Noah, Abraham, Isaac, Jacob, and Moses. It was to Moses on Mt. Sinai that the Law was given, the revealed truth of how man was to respect God, himself, and his fellow man. God dealt with the people through the prophets until the "Word was made flesh" and lived as a man among men, that is Jesus Christ, the Lord. Most people, unfortunately, concentrate on the wording of these Old Testament scriptures and think of them as negative law—all those "shall nots." It is important to remember that all the law was fulfilled in this scripture: "Love the Lord your God, with all your heart, with all your soul, and with all your might" and "Thou shalt love thy neighbor as thyself" (Mark 12:30-31). The law became a command to do, in the positive sense, and the Mosaic Law, having been fulfilled by Christ, was enunciated in a new way, replaced by faith and grace. Christ tells us how to live happy, productive lives, gives us protection and frees us from fear and ultimately teaches us how to fulfill our natures as God's finest creation on the earth. The Word gives us confidence to move forward knowing that we have a Father in Heaven who cared enough to give his only Son for us: "For God so loved the world, that he gave his only begotten Son, that whosoever believeth in him should not perish, but have everlasting life" (John 3:16).

First that which was worshipped in ignorance was made known; then it was made flesh. Now we have knowledge of God both through natural and revealed law. It is up to us not to waste this gift.

CHAPTER TWO

Natural Law, Family, and Society

God established in Genesis the first element or microcosm of society, the family. From the family, all other societal entities emanate. This principle also falls under the authority of natural law. Since we were created by God, we must obey His commands.

God created Adam and saw that he needed a companion, and just as all the rest of nature was to bring forth after its kind, so was man. Adam, Eve, and their offspring were the first community of people. From family sprang tribes, from tribes, villages, from villages, provinces, from provinces, states. Adam was the head of his household, Abraham the overseer of his, and we see the same in Jacob, whose authority devolved on his sons. Moses was the central leader of the Israelites.

It is necessary to understand that man seeks order and stability in his life. Aristotle spoke of this in his *Politics*, book I, chapter two: "the first thing to arise is the family . . . The family is the association established by nature for the supply of men's everyday wants."[1] He speaks of families uniting in villages and the state arising from these villages, then continues, "And therefore, if the earlier forms of society are natural, so is the state, for it is the end of them, and the nature of a thing, is its end. For what each thing is when fully developed, we call its nature, whether we are speaking of a man, a horse, or a family. Hence, it is evident that the state is a creation of nature, and that man is by nature a political animal."[2]

To prevent us from thinking that the state is the pinnacle of order and that the final authority rests in man, it must be remembered that not only did God establish the family, but he established kingdoms as well as their leadership. Saul, of the Tribe of Benjamin, was the first king of Israel, followed by David and his son, Solomon. Saul was anointed by Samuel at the instruction of God: "And when Samuel saw Saul, the Lord said unto him, Behold the man whom I spake to thee of! This same shall reign over my people" (Samuel I, 9:17).

Later, when David had opportunity to kill Saul, he would not: "And he said unto his men, "The Lord forbid that I should do this thing unto my master, the Lord's anointed, to stretch forth mine hand against him, seeing he is the anointed of the Lord" (Samuel I, 24:6).

Saul was God's chosen. God did not choose only from the house of Israel, but from among the Gentiles, too. In Isaiah 41:2-4 we have one of eight prophesies concerning Cyrus, king of Persia: "Who raised up the righteous man from the east, called him to his foot, gave the nations before him, and make him rule over kings? he gave them as the dust to his sword, and as driven stubble to his bow. He pursued them, and passed safely; even by the way that he had not gone with his feet. Who hath wrought and done it, calling the generations from the beginning? I the Lord, the first, and with the last; I am he."

Then in Isaiah 44:28 he is actually called by name in advance of his birth: "That saith of Cyrus, He is my shepherd, and shall perform all my pleasure: even saying to Jerusalem, Thou shalt be built; and to the temple, Thy foundation shall be laid."

Continuing in Isaiah 45:1-3 and 45:13: "Thus saith the Lord to his anointed, to Cyrus, whose right hand I have holden, to subdue nations before him; and I will loose the loins of kings, to open before him the two-leaved gates; and the gates shall not be shut; I will go before thee and make the crooked places straight: I will break in pieces the gates of brass, and cut in sunder the bars of iron: And I will give thee the treasures of darkness, and hidden riches of secret places, that thou mayest know that I, the Lord, which call thee by thy name, am the God of Israel." "I have raised him up in righteousness, and I will direct all his ways: he shall build my city, and he shall let go my captives, not for price nor reward, saith the Lord of hosts."

Isaiah the prophet lived during the reign of Hezekiah, king of Judah. According to Josephus, and as verified by the history of the destruction of the Temple, Isaiah wrote his book about 182 years before Cyrus even became king. It is interesting to note that Cyrus was called "God's shepherd" by the Greek philosopher Xenophon as well as Isaiah.

Now we know that natural law not only regulates the motion of the creation but also the society of men through the civil law as established first in the family. This is a truth that crosses geographical borders and cultural barriers. God's Law, Power, and Presence are for everyone. His word affirms that this is so in Romans 1:18-20: "For the wrath of God is revealed from heaven against all ungodliness and unrighteousness of men, who hold the truth in unrighteousness; Because that which may be known of God is manifest in them; for God hath shewed it unto them. For the invisible things of him from the creation of the world are clearly seen, being understood by the things that are made, even his eternal power and Godhead; so that they are without excuse."

The ancient Greeks provide an excellent example of knowledge of God's laws without access to His written Word and prove that it is possible for anyone, in any culture, to come to God. This is not to say, of course, that God's actual teachings can be bypassed. Paul, the apostle to the Gentiles, made this distinction when he visited Athens, the home of the ancient philosophers. He gave what is considered to be one of the most reasoned presentations ever made. It is at once brief and eloquent:

> Then Paul stood in the midst of Mars hill, and said, Ye men of Athens, I perceive that in all things ye are too superstitious. For as I passed by, and beheld your devotions, I found an altar with this inscription, To The Unknown God. Whom therefore ye ignorantly worship, him declare I unto you. God that made the world and all things therein, seeing that he is Lord of heaven and earth, dwelleth not in temples made with hands; Neither is worshipped with men's hands, as though he needed any thing, seeing he giveth to all life, and

breath, and all things; And hath made of one blood all nations of men for to dwell on all the face of the earth, and hath determined the times before appointed, and the bounds of their habitation; That they should seek the Lord, if haply they might feel after him, and find him, though he be not far from every one of us: For in him we live, and move, and have our being; as certain also of your own poets have said, For we are also his offspring. Forasmuch then as we are the offspring of God, we ought not to think that the Godhead is like unto gold, or silver, or stone, graven by art and man's device. And the times of this ignorance God winked at; but now commandeth all men every where to repent: Because he hath appointed a day, in the which he will judge the world in righteousness by that man whom he hath ordained; whereof he hath given assurance unto all men, in that he hath raised him from the dead (Acts 17:22-31).

Worship is part of man's nature and has been throughout history. Some have worshipped through faith as revealed in the Testaments, and some through ignorance, but the impulse to worship is God given and necessary. The unfortunate aspect of this is, however, that man does not always worship the Creator but rather that which was created.

God's reality remains whether or not we choose to acknowledge the hand of the Creator. He has established and ordained each element of His creation for a specific purpose. He has created order, reason, and truth to guide us, protect us, and to give us pleasure, with the ultimate end that we return home to Him. Remember, Aristotle said, "the nature of a thing, is its end." Our true nature is this: we are children of God, and our end upon this earth is to return home to the Father.

CHAPTER THREE

The Birth of Christ and the Rebirth of Man

The understanding and the appreciation of Natural Law did not end with the Ancient World, but found its fullness in the Christ. Whereas the ancients knew God by the universe and the Mosaic Law, the reality of a natural law for the soul of man was pronounced and fulfilled by the Word (that is, the Christ) through the New Testament as given by the inspiration of the Holy Spirit. All that man needed for his fulfillment and salvation was now made known through spiritual law.

Augustus Caesar was the ruler of most of the western world at the time of Christ's birth. Because of strong authoritarian rule, the Roman world was relatively peaceful and stable. Roman citizens could travel the empire in ease and safety. Commerce and trade flourished. These orderly conditions also helped Christianity to grow and flourish across the Empire. Paul the Apostle, for instance, was able as a citizen of Rome to journey to Galatia (Turkey), Greece, and, at the end of his travels, to Rome.

Roman rulers were not only the absolute rulers of civil law but were the heads of the state religion, holding the title Pontifex Maximus ("head priest"). And so, in Rome spiritual authority collided with temporal, or worldly, authority. The way early Christians responded to this collision provided an example that later gave men the will and courage to rebel against centralized rule, both temporal and spiritual.

The churches of the New Testament were autonomous and self-governing, having no centralized ruler. Each group chose leaders who met the qualifications specified in Timothy I, 3:1-10:

> A bishop then must be blameless, the husband of one wife, vigilant, sober, of good behaviour, given to hospitality, apt to teach; Not given to wine, no striker, not greedy of filthy lucre; but patient, not a brawler, not covetous; One that ruleth well his own house, having his children in subjection with all gravity; (For if a man know not how to rule his own house, how shall he take care of the church of God?)

The apostles Peter and Paul warned that there would be those who would depart from the simplicity and purity of the gospel and introduce alien practices and heresies into the church. Gnostic mysticism (secret knowledge) and unscriptural church government were already manifesting during the lives of the apostles. They warned in Peter II, 2:1, "But there were false prophets also among the people, even as there shall be false teachers among you, who privily shall bring in damnable heresies, even denying the Lord that bought them and bring upon themselves swift destruction."

In the years between the death of the apostles and the reign of the emperor Constantine, a church hierarchy was slowly set in place. Roman government did not establish this hierarchy or central government of the church. When Constantine became linked to Christianity, he used what had already come to exist.

It was not until Emperor Constantine's removal of civil government to Constantinople that the title of Pontifex Maximus was conferred on the Bishop at Rome. The "church" now began to assume the power of the Roman Empire, as evidenced by history. To the churches that arose from the teaching and instruction of the apostles, this centralized church government, was totally foreign, alien, and contrary to scripture.

Each congregation had its own elders and deacons, who constituted their governing body. Each congregation was a union of believers who came together with a belief in God and the divinity of His Son, Jesus Christ. There was no compulsion. It was a decision by each person out of his own free will, without state-prescribed authority. It was a decision based on internals, not externals, without threat of punishment. This freedom of thought and action did not last. The Christianity of the New Testament came under the compulsion of state, and teachings that were to be freely accepted or rejected were perverted into an instrument of force, a situation that would last until the fourteenth century.

The state's denial of Christianity's foundation in freedom gives new meaning to the term "dark ages." Even though the very essence of Christ's gift to mankind was that through Him individual men could know God, the interpretation of the Word was left to a few who were considered more intelligent and wise. Freedom to understand, accept, or reject the Gospel of Christ was suppressed by the state church. The equality of man before God was subjugated by the arrogance of a few; the very equality that the scriptures enunciated was denied: "There is neither Jew nor Greek, there is neither bond nor free, there is neither male nor female: for ye are all one in Christ Jesus" (Galatians 3:28).

Ultimately, the wheel came full circle. The civil government, instead of compelling religion, became the enforcer of centralized and authoritarian religion, in direct opposition to the Scriptures. Kings, princes, and governments sought the approbation of the religious authority at Rome. The results at best were confusing and at worst, cruel; people vied for power through corrupted political practices, and religion was perverted by the excesses and vanity of man. The Gospel was ignored.

The beginnings of release from this tyranny came through the aegis of John Wycliffe in the 1380s. In *History of the Puritans* (1731), Daniel Neal calls Wycliffe "the morning-star of the Reformation." It was Wycliffe who, assisted by Nicholas Hereford and John Purvey, undertook the translation of the Bible into the language of the people. The work was not completed until after his death. At last men could examine the scriptures and "know whether what his priest was telling him had the warrant of the great revelation upon which all claimed to rest."[1]

The state fought to retain its control over religion. More than twenty-five years after Wycliffe's death, in 1415 the Council of Constance issued a decree against him. Wycliffe had written "nearly two hundred volumes, all of which were called in, condemned, and ordered burned with his bones, by the Council of Constance . . . in the year 1425, forty-one years after his death."[2] After ten years of judgement, the Latin Church thought it had finally destroyed this man and his work, but new thinkers emerged; Tyndale, Luther, Knox, Zwengli, and Calvin quickly followed in Wycliffe's footsteps, each becoming integral to the sixteenth-century movement that would be known as the Reformation.

The nature of man to seek truth, to learn by his own intellect and power of reasoning—his yearning for the freedom of his conscience to understand and know the perfect will of God—had been unshackled. This new spirit of freedom was characteristic of both the Reformation and the Renaissance ("rebirth"), and the two movements evolved naturally together. For example, the printing press, invented in 1440, is viewed as a cornerstone of both historical movements. It made widespread education and great literature possible; it also enabled the translated Word of God to be available to all men everywhere. The spirit of inquiry, investigation, and learning had been reborn.

Since God had given man ability to know and learn His Law directly, it was wrong for man, no matter how intelligent, wise, or learned he appeared, to hinder the acquisition of knowledge and wisdom of another: "Woe unto you, lawyers! for ye have taken away the key of knowledge: ye entered not in yourselves, and them that were entering in ye hindered" (Luke 11:52). Since this is true for spiritual knowledge, it is true concerning the knowledge of the rest of God's creation and is but a natural extension of the freedom and responsibility of man. This revival of learning burst upon the world with brilliance, giving us not only the great reformers but Galileo, Copernicus, Newton, Bacon, Columbus, Kepler, Michelangelo, Leonardo da Vinci, and Machiavelli. Many of these men suffered greatly for the freedom to explore the universe, the arts, and the nature of government, their pursuit of the revealed laws of God that encompassed everything. In this spirit of reaching out to truth, man, who had always been accustomed to a tie "between church and state, religion and law . . . understood the Lutheran [Reformation] doctrine to apply to law as well as religion and [has] considered himself as much at liberty to determine what law he would obey as what creed he would believe."[3]

With the introduction and study of the Bible, the desire for freedom and liberty extended beyond the Roman Church, and the ideal of liberty led to resistance against the Holy Roman Empire by the German states. "In the Swiss cantons directed by Ulrich Zwingli" from "the city of Zurich" came a "plan for throwing off the sovereignty of the Empire in the Swiss cantons, republicanizing their governments, and forming them into a confederation."[4] Democracy was taking form, based on the principles of rule in the early church.

Freedom in Christ was producing greater liberty than the world had ever seen. Because governing powers had deprived men of the Word, man had lived in hopelessness and servitude in their earthly lives. The relevance of the Scriptures was now being seen in man's daily life, not only in his spiritual life. The Reformation and the Renaissance manifested the spiritual nature of man in his physical world.

CHAPTER FOUR

The Puritan Quest for Freedom

When seeking an understanding of our nation's foundation, it is natural to ask what forces shaped its founders: What drove the Puritans to the North American continent? Author George Willison tells us that "All of Europe had been in ferment for more than a century—ever since that fateful day in 1517 when Martin Luther had nailed his ninety-five theses to the door of Wittenberg Cathedral, blasting the autocratic pretensions of the Holy See and its notorious 'abuses.' His bold defiance of the Pope, the overlord of Europe, still the King of Kings, shook Christendom to its foundations, releasing and giving direction to powerful latent forces that soon swept the continent in the great revolutionary movement known as the Reformation."[1]

In the late 1500s and 1600s, the Protestant Reformation, led by Luther and Calvin, brought about a revolt against the National Church of England, which was itself struggling against Roman rule. The monarchy established supremacy over the church. Beginning in 1535, monasteries were secularized and confiscated. This action was carried out by the Earl of Essex, Thomas Cromwell, on behalf of Henry VIII. Approximately 1200 English monastic houses, which owned enormous landed estates, were secularized and distributed to the aristocracy. In this way, the king secured his support from the landed, upper-class proprietors of England. The income and jurisdiction formerly belonging to the Roman See over England passed to the Monarchy. The first English Prayer Book appeared in 1549 under Edward VI. This young king died in 1553, and a return to Roman authority was established by Mary with her marriage to Philip II of Spain.

Parliament passed a statute that instituted punishment for heresy. Bishops Ridley, Cramer, and Latimer were burned at the stake. Under Elizabeth I, royal supremacy once again was established, and under the Uniformity Act, church attendance on Sunday was obligatory under penalty of a money payment. Mary Tudor, Charles I, and James II all tried to impose their will upon the religious consciences of the people. Fortunately, the people were not timid souls to be led astray by the powers of men. Past martyrs had been their example, forerunners such as Patrick Hamilton, George Wishart, and even John Knox, who had been a galley slave for two years because of his rebellion against the papacy rule. His release came, due to the efforts of Henry VIII's son and successor, Edward VI. Knox survived Mary of Scotland and Mary Tudor, dying in 1572. The free men of Scotland had fought a hard fight, suffered much, and survived. There was no going back to denial of conscience or freedom.

This drama playing out in England had consequences for the New World as well. A revolution in thought was changing man's perception. The words of God and Christ had taken on new meaning; the seeds of freedom, coupled with the responsibility of man to God and to his fellow man, were springing forth in all their glory. "Yes," writes Willison, "the true King of Kings, that is, Christ, had shaken the false traditions of man and they were tumbling all over Europe, but with results unexpected in England. Henry VIII had his personal problems with the Papacy, namely his wife, Catherine of Aragon. It suited his personal needs to support reform, but this support of reform gave him more problems. The people were moved beyond freedom of conscience from Rome and extended this freedom of conscience to all who would dictate or suppress their rights to independence of judgement in religious matters, to freedom of conscience."[2]

The king was unwilling to grant his subjects religious freedom, and as a result, Christians were once again made martyrs for Christ. I Timothy, 2:5 told them they were right to deny their king's right to dictate their manner of worship: "For there is one God, and one mediator between God and men, the man Christ Jesus." The people became determined to return to the scriptures and to depart from the traditions of men. They wanted the purity of the gospel message. The Puritans, so called because of their desire to purify the National Church of England, wanted "purity in the worship of God and in the administration of Christ's ordinances."[3]

"A company of Puritans who ventured to meet for worship in their own way (1567), found that there were penalties for the non conforming laity as well as for non conforming clergymen"[4] Many were imprisoned, and their assemblies were forbidden. Elizabeth wanted "absolute uniformity of belief."[5] It was said that her worship services differed from the Roman Church only in language.[6] New suppressions occurred—Puritans were fined, imprisoned, and even burned at the stake. Life was not easy for those who believed that the Word of God was the final authority. The Puritans had not sought to destroy the national church, but more radical reform was imperative in order to return to the simplicity of the gospels. It was realized that the ecclesiastico-political institution called "the Church of England" was not at all a church in any New Testament meaning of the word but was (as their experience had proved) a positively anti-Christian institution."[7]

The central issues of this confrontation between the Scriptures and the state included uniformity of belief; compulsory communion in an official church; and freedom of judgment to discern the teaching of the scriptures to their application. There was also disagreement over whether the people had to accept ministers, good or bad, or whether individual congregations had right of choice; it was a question of who "rightfully spoke for" the church, "the great body of believers or a priesthood appointed from above and quite beyond the control of those below." Was "'the true' church a democratic or an autocratic institution"?[8] "Where in the Scripture, they asked, did one find rectors, vicars, deans, chaplains, chancellors, archdeacons, prebendaries, or bishops? . . . . The only lawful form of the church" it was argued, "was simplicity itself," a "priesthood of believers."[9]

These were the thoughts of Robert Browne, whose beliefs became very important to those who had moved beyond purification of a national church and had begun searching for the purity of the Scriptures, "without tarrying for any."[10] They became pilgrims, for their persecution was great. The inscription on a memorial plaque at Scrooby, north of Nottingham, England, charts their journey: "William Brewster from 1588 to 1608 and where he organized the Pilgrim Church of which he became the ruling elder, and with which, in 1608, he removed to Amsterdam, in 1609 to Leyden, and in 1620 to Plymouth where he died April 16, 1644."[11]

The pilgrims' final place of refuge was on the shores of Plymouth Rock, New England. It was there, in what is now Massachusetts, that their dream for freedom from ecclesiastical and governmental control became a reality. During the voyage upon the small *Mayflower*, troubles erupted, and it was deemed necessary to write a statement of beliefs that would govern and guarantee their freedoms; it was called the "Mayflower Compact," and it exemplified the will of free men coming together in unity. It stated:

> In the name of God, Amen. We whose names are underwritten, the loyall subjects of our dread soveraigne Lord, King James . . .doe by these presents solemnly and mutualy in the presence of God, and one of another, covenant and combine ourselves togeather into a civill body politick . . . and by vertue hearof to enacte, constitute, and frame such just and equall lawes, ordinances, acts, constitutions, and offices, from time to time, as shall be thought most meete and convenient for ye generall good of ye Colonie, unto which we promise all due submission and obedience.[12]

The compact was signed by John Carver, William Bradford, Winslow, Brewster, Allerton, Standish, Deacon Fuller, Christopher Martin, William Mullins, William White, Richard Warren, and Stephen Hopkins, among others whose names are less noteworthy. The year was 1620. What Aristotle had written of before the time of Christ had come into existence: "a very great multitude cannot be orderly; to introduce order into the unlimited is the work of a divine power . . . of such a power as holds together the universe."[13]

Democracy, modeled on the church of Christ as described in the New Testament and as embodied in the philosophy of John Locke, had begun on American shores. That men could come together in unity of purpose, their individuality and diversity as human beings recognized, attests to the truth of the Word: "For as the body is one, and hath many members, and all the members of that one body, being many, are one body: so also is Christ" (I Corinthians, 12:12).

If man would come together through unity in Christ to worship, could not they come together through their God-given free will to achieve a civil unity, not by compulsion of external forces, but by well-ordered and reasoning minds? For the autonomous and self-governing congregations of the first-century church, the Bible was the guide for their lives, spiritual and civil. They were like the worshippers described in Peter I, 2:9: "But ye are a chosen generation, a royal priesthood, an holy nation, a peculiar people; that ye should shew forth the praises of him who hath called you out of the darkness into his marvelous light."

"Peculiar," as defined by W. E. Vine, meant "a purchased possession," or "God's own possession."[14] The pilgrims sought God's governance as the author of their freedom, submitting their will to His. Individually and collectively, they owed their existence to Him and wanted *all* things in accordance with the scriptures and will of God. The movement to acknowledge God in all the comings and goings of man became an increasingly important factor in man's reasoning and thought. Thomas Hooker in the colonies and John Locke in England became very important as mankind moved forward toward the light of freedom.

Although the physical manifestations of this understanding of a new type of civil polity were occurring on the shores of North America, the search for truth was not at rest in England. While the colonies were taking root here and those earnest pilgrims were bringing forth unencumbered liberty, many of the faithful had remained behind, continuing the effort to purify the state church. One such group became known as "the Covenanters." Some of these Puritans suffered treatment not unlike the Christians under Nero in the first century. On February 28, 1638, they agreed upon a National Covenant that "condemned the King's new prayer book and ruled that the King had no power to control the Kirk [church]. The office of bishop was abolished."[15] The Puritans would have nothing to do with the English style of church government, in which Bishops ruled the people.

The Earl of Argyll raised an army of Covenanters that included General Alexander Leslie. It was not an army without support, for the women helped to fortify Leith by "carrying earth and stones" to the "defense of the port." In the interval, the Covenanters had already taken the castles at Edinburgh, Stirling, and Dumbarton. Subsequently, a truce was signed. In 1643 they pledged their aid to the English Parliament by a "Solemn League and Covenant under the promise that the Anglican Church would be reformed. The Covenanters took part in the English Civil War and finally received the surrender of Charles I in 1646. The King agreed to the covenant and the Scots fought with him against the English Parliamentary Forces. In 1650 the Covenanters were defeated by the English.

In 1660, when the monarchy was restored, the martyrdom of the Covenanters began. It lasted for twenty-five years, punctuated by rebellions in 1666, 1679, and 1685. The rebellion of 1666 was crushed at Rullion Green. Thirty members of this Covenanter Army were hanged in Edinburgh. The 1680s were known as "the Killing Times." Banishment was common, confiscation of property the rule, and trial before Sir George MacKenzie, the Lord Advocate, was feared. He was nicknamed "Bloody MacKenzie" with justification. Many were hanged after being led to their executions singing hymns or preaching to the crowd. Their monument stands in the Grey friar's churchyard, attesting to their "glorifying God in the Grassmarket."[16]

Thomas Hooker had been a minister in England, but because of threats of government sanctions against his preaching and his person, he finally arrived in the Massachusetts Colony in 1633, by way of Holland. Hooker was one of the founders of Harvard University, and in 1636 he led a group to found the Connecticut Colony and Hartford, where he served as minister until his death in 1647. He is considered by many to be the "father of American Democracy." He was an ardent spokesman for the voting rights of man in order to select the "magistrates" who would have authority over them. Mr. Hooker gave a lecture on Thursday, May 31, 1638, the truths of which were incorporated into the Fundamental Orders of Connecticut.[17] As the U.S. Constitution would be based on the Connecticut document, Hooker's influence has proven enormous. Here is a deciphered abstract of his sermon:

> Deuteronomy 1:13: "Take you wise men, and understanding, and known among your tribes, and I will make them rulers over you...."

captains over thousands, and captains over hundreds—over fifties—over tens."

Whys:
  I. That the choice of public magistrates belongs unto the people by God's own allowance.
  II. The privilege of election which belongs unto the people, therefore, must not be exercised according to their humors, but according to the blessed will and law of God.
  III. They who have power to appoint officers and magistrates, it is their power, also, to set the bounds of the power and place unto which they call them.

The lesson taught is threefold:
  I. There is matter of thankful acknowledgment in the (appreciation) of God's faithfulness towards us and the permission of these measures that God doth commend and vouchsafe.
  II. Of reproof—to dash the conceits of all those that shall oppose it.
  III. Of exhortation—to persuade us as God hath given us liberty, to *take* it.

And lastly. As God hath spared our lives, and given us them in liberty, so to seek the guidance of God, and to choose *in* God and *for* God.

The doctrine was adapted to the time, but its message was nonetheless a novelty in politics. Dr. Badon says of it: "That sermon by Thomas Hooker from the pulpit of the First Church in Hartford, is the earliest known suggestion of a fundamental law, enacted not by royal charter, nor by concession from any previously existing government, but by the people themselves—a primary and supreme law by which the government is constituted, and which not only provides for the free choice of magistrates by the people, but also sets the bounds and limitations of the power and place to which each magistrate is called."

Hooker's influence was indeed stamped upon our civil government. He would also be frequently quoted by John Locke. In 1667 Locke, the son of a Puritan-inspired lawyer, became politically motivated and acted as friend, doctor, and advisor to Lord Ashley, Chancellor of the Exchequer and "lord protector" of Carolina. It was at this time that Locke wrote the *Fundamental Constitutions for the Government of Carolina*. In 1675 Locke went for four years to France, where he wrote *The Letter Concerning Toleration*. In 1690 *The Treatises on Civil Government* were published.

Locke said in *Toleration:* "I esteem it above all things necessary to distinguish exactly the business of civil government from that of religion and to settle the just bounds that lie between the one and the other . . . .The Commonwealth seems to me to be a society of men constituted only for the procuring, preserving, and advancing their own civil interests. Civil interests I call life, liberty, health, and indolency of body, and the possessions of outward things, such as money, lands, houses, furniture, and the like."

Locke also said in *Toleration* that the "care of souls is not committed to the civil magistrate," because "it appears not that God has ever given any such authority to one man over another . . . the care of souls cannot belong to the civil magistrate, because his power consists only in outward force; but true and saving religion consists in the inward persuasion of the mind, without which nothing can be acceptable to God." Locke says it is man's responsibility "by reasoning, to draw him [the individual] into the truth."[18]

John Locke's writing reflected the tenor of the times and the principles behind the pilgrims' quest. The seeds of our constitution are contained within *Toleration*, and its understanding is found in his *Second Treatise of Civil Government*. Some excerpts from his work will illustrate the movement toward democracy and liberty that was underway, as well as the spirit from which that movement arose.

> From *Of the State of Nature,* chapter II:
>
> ". . . all men are naturally in, and that is, a state of perfect freedom to order their actions and dispose of their possessions and persons as they think fit, within the bounds of the law of Nature, without asking leave or depending upon the will of any other man."
>
> "This equality of men by Nature, . . . makes it the foundation of that obligation to mutual love amongst men on which he builds the duties they owe one another, and from whence he derives the great maxims of justice and charity."
>
> "But though this be a state of liberty, yet it is not a state of license . . . .that being all equal and independent, no one ought to harm another in his life, health, liberty or possessions."

"In transgressing the law of Nature, the offender declares himself to live by another rule than that of reason and common equity, which is that measure God has set to the actions of men for their mutual security, and so he becomes dangerous to mankind."

From *Of the State of War,* chapter III:
"I have no reason to suppose that he who would take away my liberty would not, when he had me in his power, take away everything else."

From *Of Property,* chapter V:
"every man has a property in his own person. This nobody has any right to but himself. The labor of his body and the work of his hands, we may say are properly his. . . . and did not belong in common to others."

"God, when He gave the world in common to all mankind, commanded man also to labor, and the penury of his condition required it of him."

From *Of Paternal Power,* chapter VI:
"Adam and Eve, and after them all parents were, by the law of Nature, under an obligation to preserve, nourish and educate the children they had begotten, not as their own workmanship, but the workmanship of their own Maker, the Almighty, to whom they were to be accountable for them."

"The power, then, that parents have over their children arises from that duty which is incumbent on them, to take care of their offspring during the imperfect state of childhood. To inform the mind, and govern the actions of their yet ignorant nonage, till reason shall take its place and ease them of that trouble, *is what the children want, and the parents are bound to.*"

"The nourishment and education of their children is a charge so incumbent on parents for their children's good, that *nothing can absolve* them from taking care of it."

From *Of Political or Civil Society,* chapter VII:
"Man . . . hath by nature a power not only to preserve his property—that is, his life, liberty, and estate, against the injuries and attempts of other men, but to judge of, and punish the breaches of that

law in others, as he is persuaded the offence deserves, even with death itself, in crimes where the heinousness of the fact, in his opinion, requires it."

From *Of the Extent of the Legislative Power,* chapter XI:
"the first fundamental positive law of all commonwealths is the establishing of the legislative power."

"Secondly, . . .the legislative or supreme authority cannot assume to itself a power to rule by extemporary arbitrary decrees, but is bound to dispense justice and decide the rights of the subject by promulgated standing laws."

"Thirdly, the supreme power cannot take from any man any part of his property without his own consent."

From *Of the Dissolution of Government,* chapter XIX:
"The end of government is the good of mankind; and which is best for mankind, that the people should be always exposed to the boundless will of tyranny, or that the rulers should be sometimes liable to be opposed when they grow exorbitant in the use of their power, and employ it for the destruction, and not the preservation, of the properties of their people?"

"Who shall be judge whether the legislative act contrary to their trust? . . .The people shall be judge; . . . by having deputed him, have still a power to discard him when he fails in his trust?"

Although Locke's work was in accord with the times, it was also very radical, in that he claimed that princes did not inherit the right to rule, according to the full understanding of the theory of natural law, wherein all men were equal and had the natural right of the consent of the governed. Locke was befriended by William Penn when he was falsely accused of writing tracts against the government during the reign of James II; still, he endured exile in Holland. He returned to England when William and Mary ascended the throne in 1688.[19]

Locke's works *Essay on Human Understanding, The Reasonableness of Christianity, The Treatises on Civil Government,* and *A Letter Concerning Toleration* were widely read from the continent to the colonies. What Hooker had begun, Locke was enlarging for the good of all mankind. In the colonies, where he had seen the results of Hooker's beliefs and his theories so logically presented, the *Treatise on Civil Government* became the bedrock from which sprang revolution and union. It was Locke who established, through an appeal to the reason of Natural Law Theory under God, that all men had the "right to life, liberties, and possessions" [20] It was the final chapter of the *Treatise* that gave the justification for the Declaration of Independence, and Locke's work as a whole found fertile ground in the minds of the colonists, inspiring them to insist upon the inclusion of the Bill of Rights in the United States Constitution. Those basic rights were ratified in 1791. The principles of Hooker expanded by Locke were no longer theory, but rather were embodied in a nation whose future would be determined by the will of its people.

CHAPTER FIVE

The Spirit of the Revolution and Constitution

The colonies of Jamestown and Plymouth were the beginnings of a constant influx of people seeking a better life, a life predicated on freedom and hope. The repression of individual freedoms had not ended in Europe, and people were willing to risk their lives and their futures for the mere hope of a better tomorrow, a future without faceless tyrants and impersonal, oppressive governments dictating every facet of their lives. They came as free men and women or as indentured servants; some came with the financial support of their families, and others arrived with their earthly goods upon their backs, but all came with hope. They had courage and faith in their abilities to achieve their goals using their individual talents and initiatives, dependent upon no one but God and themselves to sustain them through the difficult times.

The colonies and their growing populations prospered, perhaps too much. The more successful the colonists were, the greater the taxation burdens they were made to shoulder. English rulers, supported by a willing Parliament, were quick to pass any legislation or measures that would enrich the government's coffers, so the colonists' success was legally penalized and their property plundered. When one considers the various taxes and trade restrictions imposed and the outrageous reasoning used to justify it, one marvels that the colonists were patient for more than a hundred years. Here is an overview of the taxation and restrictions suffered by the colonies:

THE NAVIGATION ACT OF 1660: Charles II, September 13, 1660. Restricted imports and exports.

THE NAVIGATION ACT OF 1663: Charles II, July 27, 1663. Further trade restrictions to ensure "a firmer dependence" on England.

THE NAVIGATION ACT OF 1696: William III, April 10, 1696. Search and seizure laws affecting trade.

THE WOOLEN ACT OF 1699: William III, May 4, 1699. Protectionist laws for English woolen industry. No wool to be exported.

THE HAT ACT OF 1732: George II, June 1, 1732. Protectionist laws for the English hat industry. No exportation of "hats or felts" by the colonies.

THE MOLASSES ACT OF 1733: George II, May 17, 1733. Taxation and duties placed upon "rum and spirits of the produce or manufacture any of the colonies" as well as molasses, syrups, and sugars.

THE IRON ACT OF 1750: George II, April 12, 1750. Restricted the manufacture of steel and the erection of any "mill, engine, forge, furnace" with a penalty of two hundred pounds. Again, another protectionist law.

THE REVENUE ACT OF 1764: George III, April 5, 1764. Trade duties on imports and exports. Protectionism was no longer offered as an excuse. Money for the English government and the British Crown was the admitted reason for this tax.

THE STAMP ACT OF 1765: George III, 1765. Revenue was to go directly into his Majesty's Exchequer from the duties levied The pretense and hiding behind fancy words and contrived reasons was finished.

THE QUARTERING ACT OF 1765: George III, May 15, 1765. Enforced housing and feeding of British soldiers and officers by the colonies.

THE DECLARATORY ACT OF 1766: George III, March 18, 1766. All laws passed by the colonies for their benefit and protection were rendered null and void by the Crown and Parliament. The colonies were to be "subordinate to" and "dependent upon" the

"Crown and the Parliament of Great Britain." All that had been tolerated had finally led to their now feudal condition. They had become the slaves of a corrupt and greedy government.

THE REVENUE ACT OF 1767: THE TOWNSHEND ACT: George III, June 26, 1767. Additional duties imposed for the support of government personnel in the colonies with search and seizure ordered. The colonists had been so restricted in their trade that the British realized that goods they had declared illegal were most certainly in the possession of many and they saw this as an opportunity to raise even more money.

ACT SUSPENDING NEW YORK ASSEMBLY: George III, July 2, 1767. This was a forceful restatement of the Declaratory Act with New York bearing the full brunt of the law.

RESOLVES OF PARLIAMENT AND ADDRESS TO THE KING, 1769: George III, February 9, 1769. This act was in response to Massachusetts' desire to hold a convention with elected representatives from other colonies. It was said to be an "audacious usurpation" of government. A special commission was instituted to find the perpetrators and punish their offence.

THE BOSTON PORT ACT, 1774: George III, March 31, 1774 (First "Intolerable Act"). Armed soldiers and officers were placed on all ships at the port of Salem before proceeding to Boston Harbor. Nothing could enter Boston until full restitution had been made to the East India Company by or for the citizens of Boston.

THE MASSACHUSETTS GOVERNMENT ACT, 1774: George III, May 20, 1774 (Second "Intolerable Act"). All law was put into the hands of government appointees. The right to assemble was denied.

THE ADMINISTRATION OF JUSTICE ACT OF 1774: George III, May 20, 1774. (Third "Intolerable Act"). In this act, the magistrates would not face trial in the Colony of Massachusetts if an indictment or accusation was made. They were not to face a jury comprised of the citizens of Massachusetts. This left no restraint on the magistrates of the British government in their dealings with the people. Theft and violence against the people could and was disguised as lawful acts against the people. The citizens had lost all means of lawful defense against a government that had made them de facto slaves.

QUARTERING ACT OF 1774: George III, June 2, 1774 (Fourth "Intolerable Act"). Simply put, under this act, the government could take almost any property it chose in order to house the officers and soldiers of the government.[1]

In examining the chronology of the British legislation for the colonies, it is important to notice that the oppression began very slowly, with much "apparent" justification. The New Deal, the Great Society, and the new "politics of meaning" are modern examples of this same old formula of government greed posing as government generosity. The Parliament was no Robin Hood. It stole from the people legally—and gave the spoils to those who were already rich or who lusted after pure, unadulterated power. Creeping taxation (the kind we have now) climbed the hill slowly, but when it arrived at the top of the hill in 1764, it came down upon the colonies like an avalanche. The government no longer saw the rights of the citizens as something to be cherished. All they saw was a pot of gold to be endlessly mined, and when the people could no longer accept their imposed burdens, the government set out to destroy and crush the opposition.

The British government had no one to blame but themselves. George Bancroft said in his *History of the United States*, "The world was rising up against superstition and authority over the mind."[2] "Authority over the mind"; political correctness—what a horrible and meaningful phrase. Those words should strike fear and righteous anger into the hearts of all mankind. The British Crown and Parliament were trying to exercise authority over the minds of the colonists. If they couldn't be taxed into submission, then laws that denied their free exercise of thought like the second "Intolerable Act" were the order of the day.

In 1764 James Otis wrote *The Rights of the British Colonies Asserted and Proved*. He argued that any government whose foundation lay in power would "destroy all distinction between right and wrong; that it overturns all morality, and leaves it to every man to do what is right in his own eyes; that it leads directly to skepticism, and ends in atheism." In writing about the foundation of government, he reasoned that its proper foundation lay not in grace; nor on force, nor on compact, nor property:

> "Has it any solid foundation, any chief cornerstone, but what accident, chance or confusion may lay one moment and destroy the next? I think it is the everlasting will of GOD, the author of nature, whose laws never vary . . . Government is therefore most evidently founded on the necessities of our nature . . . Government is founded immediately on the necessities of human nature, and ultimately on the will of God . . . But if every prince since Nimrod had been a tyrant, it would not prove a right to tyrannize. There can be no prescription old enough to supersede the law of nature, and the grant of God almighty; who has given to all men a natural right to be free . . . if they please . . . The same law of nature and of reason is equally obligatory on a democracy, an aristocracy, and a monarchy: Whenever the administrators, in any of those forms, deviate from truth, justice and equity, they verge towards tyranny, and are to be opposed; and if they prove incorrigible, they will be deposed by the people, if the people do not prove too abject.[3]

The people of the colonies did not prove to be abject. Virginia took dead aim on the Stamp Act. Instead of suffering under the duties on trade, "articles of luxury of English manufacture were banished; and threadbare coats came into fashion."[4] The English lost a very profitable market. It is a wonderful example. The colonists weren't spoiled. They weren't bothered about keeping up with the Joneses. They were a people of principle and self-restraint, not given to unnecessary indulgence. They had the self-discipline to put matters of principle above appearances and the materialistic concerns of the world. There were more "non-importation agreements" and the English merchants suffered a loss of nearly £700,000 between 1767 and 1769. As a result of this loss, all the duties imposed by the Townshend Act of 1767, except the one on tea, were repealed in 1770.

A brief lull in political activity followed the repeal of the act. But although things seemed calm on the surface, Samuel Adams, for one, was very busy. He wrote various articles, under such names as "Candidus" and "Valerious Poplicola," for the *Boston Gazette*. His articles explained what government should be. He used the works of John Locke and Emerich de Vattel to illustrate what needed to be done.

Adams and the other founding fathers were not bent on establishing a new nation at the outset of this conflict. They were determined to keep what God had given to them and to the rest of mankind. The freedom to think, to work, to hold property, and to live in peace without the paternal hand of government interfering in every aspect of their lives with policies that were, and still are, antithetical to the laws of nature and the inherent nature of man.

Other writers joined Adams. John Dickinson's "Farmer's Letters to the Inhabitants of the British Colonies" said, "Slavery is ever preceded by sleep." Dickenson's pamphlets were widely read, circulated, and shared. All played their part, awakening and informing the citizenry. The colonists entered into voluntary communications with each other. John Fiske said "that the committees of correspondence did indeed grow into a mighty tree; for it was nothing less than the beginning of the American Union."[5]

In 1772 Samuel Adams, Joseph Warren, and Benjamin Church were chosen to write a message to the governor about "stipends" for judges. The governor responded as expected. Governor Hutchinson said it was not proper for him to show any of his correspondence as governor. When there was to be another meeting, the governor declined to let them assemble at their appointed time, as this would set a bad example to other communities and towns. His letter was read to those who had gathered. Samuel Adams then made a motion, one which the Tories called "the source of the rebellion": "That a committee of correspondence be appointed, to consist of twenty-one persons, to state the rights of the colonists . . . to communicate and publish the same to the several towns in this province and to the world . . with the infringements and violations thereof that have been, or from time to time may be made; also requesting of each town a free communication of their sentiments on this subject."[6]

The Boston letter was read far and wide, and the submerged thoughts of the people began to rise to the surface. In 1773 other colonies followed suit, appointing their own committees of correspondence. The groundwork was being laid. Finally in November of 1773, the Boston committee resolved that it was time to act. On the evening of December 16, 1773, a boat loaded with tea was boarded and the tea dumped over the side. We all know the story of the Boston Tea Party, but do we know how the people of Boston and Cambridge suffered? The punishment was the Boston Port Bill, signed March 31, 1774. It went into effect June 1, 1774, and was administered by Thomas Gage, captain general and governor of Massachusetts.

The port of Boston was closed to foreign trade and even to domestic trade. The city was under siege as surely as if they were engaged in open warfare. It was a warfare of the most important kind. The stakes were the minds of the people exercising their freedom in defiance of the control of a strong centralized government forcing its will upon them. The port was closed, jobs were lost, there were no goods to buy, and American goods could not be shipped. To the credit of the other colonies, they at once went to the aid of the Massachusetts colony, sending donations of all kinds for the relief of the citizens. Instead of breaking the will of the people, the Port Bill forged a will of iron resolve that proved to be an example of courage and steadfastness to principle for the other colonies to witness. There was fasting and prayer in the city, and a bond was created that only suffering can build. The British could not win. The colonies were united in spirit despite their diversity, and their determination strengthened them for what was to come.

The Continental Congress was convened in Philadelphia on September 3, 1774. They adopted measures to seek a redress of grievances, to petition the Crown, and to defend themselves against the denial of freedom guaranteed to subjects of Great Britain. The English Parliament made weak overtures of conciliation that were rejected by the colonists. These measures would have repealed the Boston Port Act and the Tea Tax. The Parliament refused to repeal the Massachusetts Acts, which kept the thumb of centralized government pressed on the colony permanently. John Adams wrote articles reminding the people that by nature all men were equal and that no one had the power to alter that eternal fact. Committees of safety were formed in the colonies, and the British began to stockpile arms and to disarm the Massachusetts citizens. General Gage decided that it was time to destroy the military stores that the people had collected at Concord. Riders were sent to warn the colonists. The date was April 19, 1775. The people gathered at Lexington near Concord. The British fired, killing some and wounding others. The British marched on toward Concord, six miles away. They encountered about a hundred men at the "old North Bridge." More citizens were killed, and the revolution was born. There was no turning back. The British troops turned toward Boston when the militia of the colony attacked. Their march to Boston became a run.

The colonists did not enter into the rebellion against England lightheartedly. England's intransigence was the ultimate cause. Their refusal to acknowledge the freedom of the colonies galvanized the future Americans to unite in their common defense and ultimately to declare their independence.

On July 6, 1775, "The Declaration of the Causes and Necessity of Taking Up Arms" was issued by the Congress of the United Colonies convened in Philadelphia. This was a definitive document. It pointed out the justice of their actions as supported by the overwhelming evidence of natural law. It was a statement of the cause of and necessity of defense, not a declaration of independence. It went so far as to state that they did "not" want "to dissolve the union" and that they "sincerely wished to see it restored." The document concluded: "With an humble confidence in the mercies of the supreme and impartial Judge and Ruler of the Universe, we most devoutly implore His divine goodness to protect us happily through this great conflict, to dispose our adversaries to reconciliation on reasonable terms, and thereby to relieve the empire from the calamities of civil war."

The British did not respond in a reasonable way; common sense had fled from the Parliament and the Crown. On June 15, 1776, George Washington had been elected commander-in-chief of the Continental Army. Throughout the last half of 1775 and the beginning of 1776, there were battles and skirmishes with the British army. As the weeks and months slipped away, it became evident that the English were never going to alter their desire to be feudal masters of the colonies and their people. As a result, the citizens of the various colonies began to speak openly of the necessity of declaring their independence from England, joining together in a union to become a nation. The consequence was a resolution passed on June 7, 1776, to form "a plan of confederation to be prepared and transmitted to the respective colonies for their consideration and approbation." This plan called for dissolving the union with and allegiance to England. Thus the committee was formed to draft the Declaration of Independence, the greatest human document ever written. The Declaration was predicated on the natural law of God and sought His protection and guidance repeatedly in the coming conflict. The promise of this relatively short document has offered hope for the millions who have sought the refuge of our nation. This one small piece of paper still remains the most stirring call to freedom in the world, a world that seeks to enslave. The document's last paragraph says: "We, therefore, the Representatives of the United States of America, in General Congress, Assembled, appealing to the Supreme Judge of the world for the rectitude of our intentions, do in the Name, and by the Authority of the good People of these Colonies, solemnly publish and declare, that these United Colonies are absolved from all Allegiance to the British Crown." George Bancroft wrote in his *History of the United States*, "As the fleets and armies of England went forth to consolidate arbitrary power, the sound of war everywhere else on the earth died away. Kings sat still in awe, and the nations turned to watch the issue."

On November 15, 1777, agreement was reached on the Articles of Confederation. Freedom was at hand. The war spanned nearly six and a half years, beginning at Concord, Massachusetts, in 1775, and lasting until the surrender of General Cornwallis at Yorktown on October 19, 1781. The peace treaties were not signed until September 3, 1783, in Paris. The British finally evacuated New York on November 25, 1783, and General Washington resigned his commission December 23, 1783, and returned to Mount Vernon.

The next step was our constitution. The Convention was convened in May of 1787, but many delegates didn't arrive until June. Getting the delegates from the diverse colonies to agree on anything was no easy task. The debates and arguments among the delegates were heated. These were men of great conviction. It was a classic case of immovable objects being confronted by irresistible forces. All sides had become intransigent. No compromise, much less any agreement, was possible. At this point, amidst this fever-pitched environment, on Thursday, June 28, 1787, during the constitutional debates, the most beautiful recognition of God came from Dr. Benjamin Franklin. Dr. Franklin rose to address the delegates:

> Mr. President, the small progress we have made after four or five weeks close attendance and continual reasoning with each other—

our different sentiments on almost every question, several of the last producing as many noes as ays, is methinks a melancholy proof of the imperfection of the Human Understanding. We indeed seem to feel our own want of political wisdom, since we have been running about in search of it. We have gone back to ancient history for models of Government, and examined the different forms of those Republics which having been formed with the seeds of their own dissolution now no longer exist. And we have viewed Modern States all round Europe, but find none of their constitutions suitable to our circumstances.

In this situation of this Assembly, groping as is were in the dark to find political truth, and scarce able to distinguish it when presented to us, how has it happened, Sir, that we have not hitherto once thought of humbly applying to the Father of lights to illuminate our understandings? In the beginning of the Contest with G. Britain, when we were sensible of danger we had daily prayer in this room for the divine protection. Our prayers, Sir, were heard, and they were graciously answered. All of us who were engaged in the struggle must have observed frequent instances of a superintending providence in our favor. To that kind providence we owe this happy opportunity of consulting in peace on the means of establishing our future national felicity. And have we now forgotten that powerful friend? Or do we imagine that we no longer need His assistance? I have lived, Sir, a long time, and the longer I live, the more convincing proofs I see of this truth—that God Governs in the affairs of men. And if a sparrow cannot fall to the ground without his notice, is it probable that an empire can rise without His aid? We have been assured, Sir, in the sacred writings, that except the Lord build the House they labour in vain that build it. I firmly believe this; and I also believe that without His concurring aid we shall succeed in this political building no better, than the Builders of Babel: We shall be divided by our little partial local interests; our projects will be confounded, and we ourselves shall become a reproach and bye word down to future ages. And what is worse, mankind may hereafter from this unfortunate instance, despair of establishing Governments by Human wisdom and leave it to chance, war and conquest. I therefore beg leave to move—that henceforth prayers imploring the assistance of Heaven, and its blessings on our deliberations, be held in this Assembly every morning before we proceed to business, and that one or more of the Clergy of this City be requested to officiate in that Service.

It cannot be argued that our founding fathers had set their minds and inclined their hearts toward God. This trust in God formed a foundation on which the conventioneers overcame their differences to draft our constitution. Are we, the inheritors of that work, destroying the foundation?

Chapter Six

Intellectual Elitism, Gnosticism, and the Great Lie

Science and civil policy are not the only factors weighing on our society. Another, crucial element has been shaping our world for centuries: man's quest for spiritual "enlightenment." This search has led people down many paths; it has taken on different appearances and inspired various doctrines, but the delusionary qualities at the heart of it remain constant. The search has even become an integral part of civil governments and religious bodies, and it has distorted science. It has not, however, succeeded in perverting natural law, because natural law cannot be destroyed or altered. This search has led people to set aside God, venerating instead "the cosmos," "the great one," the "exalted powers of the universe," vague concepts that deny the intent and inherent goodness of the creation and the Creator.

This search for "enlightenment" can generally be called "gnosticism," the spiritual delusion. Gnosticism is deceiving, artful, beguiling, and cunning—it clothes itself in light and beauty to deceive even the most learned persons. It shrouds itself in hope for the poor and weak and promises knowledge for those who seek power and wealth, all the while promising eternal life. It imitates the Light but is not the Light. How does gnosticism gain entrance into man's spiritual and material life? Through his confidence in his self-will, his belief that he is superior to others either in mind, body, or soul.

This chapter does not, by any pretense, seek to explain gnosticism completely, only to touch upon its major aspects and influences, to show it as a connecting thread between various harmful practices, an enemy with destructive power and insidious ways. Gnosticism is to be fought as strenuously as if one is defending his life against a murderer. It is the murderer of the soul.

The philosophies of men have been a stumbling block, causes of strife, racism, genocide, and persecution. People often seem to have a chip on their shoulders when "religion' is mentioned, relying upon stock answers voiced in challenging tones. The most frequently used expressions are: "That's a private matter;" "That's between God and me;" or the ultimate phrase, "More harm and pain has been caused in this world by religion than anything else." Many people don't want truth, are afraid of truth, resent truth, or worse—hate truth.

By contrast, philosophers have taken up a great quest for truth. Their search, though, has generally led them away from God, rather than toward Him. Descartes gave us duality of man; Sartre, existentialism; and Nietzsche, nihilism; but none have explained the soul or seemed to offer any hope, or find any meaning in life. Reason is a beautiful and magnificent characteristic of man, but mankind seems to have a great deal of trouble avoiding "vain and unlearned questions." When reason is followed alone, without faith, the arguments that result are inevitably lies.

All these false words and false paths proceed from one original lie. Science, the philosophies of men, and the complicated religions of the "enlightened" have served and perpetuated the original falsehood. What was this lie, this deluding destroyer of men's souls?

We learn of the lie in Genesis 3:4-5: "And the serpent said unto the Woman; Ye shall not surely die: For God doth know that in the day ye eat thereof; then your eyes shall be opened, and ye shall be as gods, knowing good and evil." The lie revealed in these verses has three parts:

    1. "Ye shall not surely die."
    2. "your eyes shall be opened and ye shall be as gods."
    3. "knowing good and evil."

Satan's first lie is obviously false, since from conception we are inexorably moving toward physical death. The second lie implied

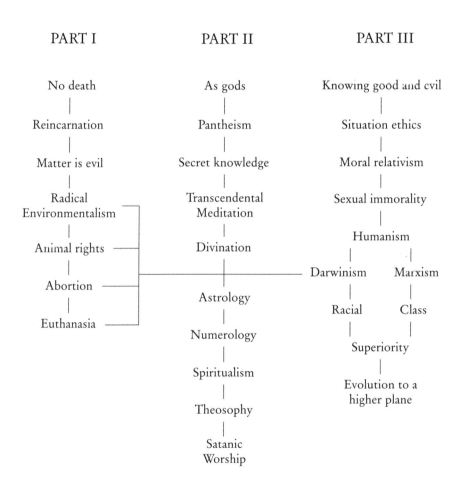

that special knowledge, gnosticism, would be given, and with that knowledge, Adam and Eve would be equal with God. The final part of the blasphemy promised that mankind would know the absolutes of good and evil and be able to decide these matters *themselves*, without the wisdom and instruction of God, their Creator.

Because of this great lie, man departed from truth, and with the exception of Noah and his family, the mass of humanity was destroyed for their wickedness. Despite God's punishment and mercy, mankind again rebelled, attempting to build a tower to reach to heaven. This time God did not destroy them. He dispersed them throughout the world, confusing their languages. Once again, man had the temerity to equate himself with God. It became a pattern. Man's rebellion became the rule, not the exception. Because of Abraham's faith, which was counted as righteous, God chose his descendants through Isaac to be the people to whom the first revealed law was given, and through his line, the blessing of salvation would come into the world in the form of the Christ living on earth as a man. That which was prophesied came to pass just as God promised.

Despite the salvation God offers, from the beginning, Satan's lie has ensnared men, deluding them and destroying their souls. When Satan said, "ye shall not surely die," he appealed to man's most basic instinct—survival. Men struggle and fight to sustain and prolong life as long as possible on earth. But man *can* have eternal life, and it is assured that he will: with God—or Satan. Life does not recycle as the Eastern religions would have us believe. One cannot be a Christian and believe in reincarnation. Why? Reincarnation by its nature denies a day of judgment; it denies righteousness and justice. In the Hindu religions, karma is the rationale for pain and suffering or riches and pleasures. Its essence, depending on your current life, permits you to be rewarded or punished in your next life. The purpose is to move upward (evolve), improving yourself in each subsequent life. However, this does not rule out going backward; according to this theory, if you were very bad, you could return with severe birth defects or as some animal. The ultimate Hindu goal is "nirvana," or the extinction of individual existence by the absorption of the soul into the "universal consciousness." In the *Star Wars* trilogy, it was called "the force." This "universal consciousness" accepts that everything, whether it is a tree, an animal, or a human being, is a soul, seeking to unite with the supreme power.

This logic leads directly to pantheism, a multiplicity of gods. That Godless framework is the basis for situation ethics, moral relativism, humanism, and the created gods of man. It justifies using "any means to an end." It creates the falsehood of "man is god," or that man can become god, and if man is god, he can do as he pleases and it will be right, even if it is only right for him. It is the second part of the great lie: "Your eyes shall be opened and ye shall be as gods."

The last part of the lie says, "knowing good and evil." Knowledge in and of itself is not evil. Knowledge is useful for guidance and discernment in living, but this is not the type of knowledge Satan promised. This is special knowledge, secret knowledge for an elite group.

True knowledge is never held in secret. In Proverbs 1:7 we are told that "the fear of the Lord is the beginning of knowledge," and in Ephesians 4:13-14, "Till we all come in the unity of the faith, and of the knowledge of the Son of God, unto a perfect man, unto the measure of the stature of the fullness of Christ: That we henceforth be no more children, tossed to and fro, and carried about with every wind of doctrine, by the sleight of men, and cunning craftiness, whereby they lie in wait to deceive."

The revealed Word of God is for all, not just a special few. It was given fully and completely, with nothing omitted, for the salvation of man. God gave His Son for all of us, openly. There was no further knowledge needed beyond that of Christ crucified and resurrected. This is the promise of salvation, not some secret or esoteric knowledge.

The New Age movement is not new. It is the great lie dressed in new clothing. Throughout the world, this has been and is known as gnosticism. It comes from the Greek *gnosis*, meaning "knowledge." Gnosticism is very difficult to understand, because it is so esoteric and complex. Its outer trappings change to fit different historical periods, but the basic premise does not change. In gnosticism, one has "knowledge" that can be gained only by being initiated into the "secret" teachings by those who are "enlightened," sometimes called "illuminati," "masters," "channelers," or "mediums." Gnosticism teaches that the cosmos is god, and we are all part of this cosmic force, alienated by matter, which is evil. Through denial of physical matter, including our own bodies, people are taught to transcend the earthly in order to seek spiritual oneness with the cosmos. This heresy is the lie that denies the good of creation, which was, in essence, the creation of matter, and gnostics believe matter to be evil. It denies the divinity of Christ and God incarnate because He lived as a man physically, in the material world. The supreme goal of gnosticism is to destroy God, and the method is to destroy His creation. Man is devalued by it, and in turn, God is devalued by man.

Gnosticism is the chameleon behind paganism and neo-paganism. It masquerades as goodness, clothed in seeming virtue, openness, piety, sacrifice, and light. We have been warned against this: "For such are false apostles, deceitful workers, transforming themselves into the apostles of Christ. And no marvel; for Satan himself is transformed into an angel of light. Therefore, it is no great thing if his ministers also be transformed as the ministers of righteousness; whose end shall be according to their works" (II Corinthians, 11:13-15).

The "great deceiver" can appear as the light to a searching world, as can those who follow his delusion. Gnosticism has authored many religious doctrines in many guises. The pantheism of Egypt is an early example; its initiations and its dualism and the cycle of birth; death, and rebirth, with the egg as its symbol, are aligned with the "recycling of life" espoused by Buddhism, Hinduism, and other Eastern religions. Before settling finally in Italy, Pythagoras, "the Master of Samos," traveled in Egypt and the East. In Egypt, he was initiated into the mysteries of Osirus and became a "master." Most of his philosophical teachings were wrapped in the metaphysics of numbers. As Pythagorean doctrine is currently understood, the soul could unite with the divine, reincarnation was shown through the mystery of numbers, and first and foremost, secrecy was necessary. Purification from the material world was necessary in order to be reunited with the power of the universe.

The common thread that binds all gnostic beliefs are symbols, such as the rainbow, light, relics, reunification with the cosmos, duality (giving evil equality with goodness in power), the manifestation of evil in matter, asceticism (self denial), life cycles, and vegetarianism. These ingredients have their genesis in Satan's lie. The terrible paradox is that the great lie itself is the recycling element in the world. God has never altered His truth, but has demonstrated through its consistency that it is the true path.

The apostles repeatedly warned against the lie. Paul said in Galatians 1:8-12, "But though we, or an angel from heaven, preach any other gospel unto you than that which we have preached unto you, let him be accursed. As we said before, so say I now again, If any man preach any other gospel unto you than that ye have received, let him be accursed. For do I now persuade men, or God? Or do I seek to please men? for if I yet pleased men, I should not be the servant of Christ. But I certify you, brethren, that the gospel, which was preached of me, is not after man. For I neither received it of man, neither was I taught it, but by the revelation of Jesus Christ." Paul's message tells us:

1. Perversion of the Gospel was occurring
2. Receive no other gospel, not even from an angel
3. Aim not to please men, but Christ
4. The Gospel was not received by Paul from men
5. The Gospel was not taught to Paul by men.

Paul and Peter spoke also of genealogies, not eating meat, not marrying, fables, and seductive doctrines. The gnosticism of the pre-Christian world was already adapting itself to meet the authority of Christ, and the heresy continued its battle, clothed in the "light" of mystery and secret knowledge.

In the Christian period, the assault on the Godhead came through the influence of pagan religions directly denying the authority of Christ himself. Manichaeism was made manifest in the third century, originating in Persia. Among Manichaean teachings were abstinence from wine, meat, and sexual intercourse. The founder of this group was named Mani. Mani viewed himself as a successor to Christ. He was called the "Apostle of Light" or the "Illuminator," and sent proselytizing missions far and wide. Augustine, in the late fourth century, was a member of this gnostic group, but renounced it in 382 A.D. After this period, Manichaeism fell back toward the Asian cultures, although it remained strong in North Africa for several centuries.

Prior to Manichaeism there were heretical gnostic sects such as those influenced by Marcion and Bardesanes. After the Manichaeans there were the Cathars, who were remnants of the crusaders from France. Having been in the East, and in Constantinople in particular, they came in contact with a gnostic group that adhered to the Bogomil Heresy, which arose from still another group, called the Paulicians, who arose in the eleventh century in Bulgaria. The Bogomil Heresy spread with minor innovations through the Balkans, Asia Minor, and Russia. They practiced a high degree of asceticism (self-denial). The Cathars had influence in southern France until the early 1400s. The Christian form of gnosticism denied the salvation through Christ, thereby denying faith and grace, relying on special or "secret" knowledge as the "light" that brings salvation. It is to be understood that reincarnation was part and parcel of this new paganism, which esposed superiority of a few who had seemingly evolved higher through previous lives.

Although he was not agnostic in the traditional sense, a review of Marx's works reveals that he was a hater of God. From his *Communist Manifesto*, we know that he wanted to destroy all religion and all morality. Marx adhered to the lie—specifically the third part, "knowing good and evil." Marx said, "The religious world is but the reflex of the real world . . . The religious reflex of the real world can . . . only then vanish when the practical relations of everyday life offer to man none but perfectly intelligent and reasonable relations with regard to his fellow men and to nature."[1]

Marx did allow that Christianity was "useful" because it forbids, in the name of religion, the same faults that the penal code condemns.[2] Marx's gnosticism saw religion only as a delusion, lacking reality. What he failed to comprehend was that the penal code was built upon the Judeo-Christian ethic. In the *Communist Manifesto* he writes, "the ancient world was overcome by Christianity," but Christianity "succumbed" to the "Rationalists" of the eighteenth century. "Undoubtedly," he continues, "religious, moral philosophical, and juridical ideas have been modified in the course of historical development. But religion, morality, philosophy, political science, and law constantly survived the change."

Marx adds, "There are, besides, eternal truths, such as Freedom, Justice, etc., that are common to all states of society. But communism abolishes eternal truths; it abolishes all religion, and all morality . . . it therefore acts in contradiction to all past historical experience."

The arrogance of the Marx's statements can only be equated

with that first great lie. Marx had become "god," an echo of the great destroyer, Satan. This was to be a "new and "higher" plane of evolution for the world. In his preface to *Das Kapital* he said, "As soon as society has outlived a given period of development, and is passing over from one given stage to another, it begins to be subject to other laws. In a word, economic life offers us a phenomenon analogous to the history of evolution in other branches of biology." This is dated 1873 and is signed, Karl Marx.

If Marxism and its offshoot, socialism, have perpetuated the lie in the social realm, Darwinism has done the same for science. Charles Darwin was not the first to entertain the theory of evolution, however. And Charles Darwin had a religious upbringing. His father, Dr. Robert Darwin, was a minister. For his vocation, however, Charles Darwin turned to science. Darwin developed the theory of evolution, which is articulated in *Origin of Species*.[3] In *Apes, Angels, and Victorians*, by Sir Julian Huxley and H. B. D. Kettlewell, we learn that Darwin's "religion had wasted away before his science in a war of attrition so gradual that in his own words, he 'felt no distress and hardly realized that a shot had been fired.'"[4] Darwin had in his works and his own mind removed God as Creator and reduced man to nothing more than a coequal member of the animal kingdom. For Darwin and his followers, man's devaluation was to have even larger significance. Bent on being master of himself, man had ironically lost his most glorious attribute; being made in the image of God, by God.

Although *Origin of Species* is probably Darwin's most famous work, *Descent of Man* is likely the most disturbing, because of conclusions drawn at the treatise's close:

> Man scans with scrupulous care the character and pedigree of his horses, cattle, and dogs before he matches them; but when he comes to his own marriage he rarely, or never, takes any such care . . . Both sexes ought to refrain from marriage if they are in any marked degree inferior in body or mind . . . Everyone does good service who aids towards this end.
>
> The advancement of the welfare of mankind is a most intricate problem; all ought to refrain from marriage who cannot avoid abject poverty for their children, . . . if the prudent avoid marriage, whilst the reckless marry, the *inferior members* tend to supplant the better *members of society*.

> We must, . . . acknowledge, . . . that man with all his noble qualities, with sympathy which feels for the most debased, with benevolence which extends not only to other men but to the humblest living creature, with his god-like intellect which has penetrated into the movements and constitution of the solar system—with all those exalted powers—man still bears in his bodily frame the indelible stamp of this lowly origin.[5]

Darwin's comparison of animal breeding to marriage is in direct conflict with our power of reasoning and intelligence. Next, he denies our equality through God, and consequently advocates birth control predicated on inferiority, poverty, or genetics. In the last paragraph he finally enunciates that we should give honor and respect to all animals because of *our lowly origins.* Most amazingly, Darwin's own gnosticism is revealed when he speaks of "all those exalted powers" of the solar system. The "powers" of the universe had become Darwin's god.

Contemporaneous with Marx and Darwin came a surge in mystical and "secret" teachings. Several groups surfaced, calling themselves by such titles as the Theosophical Society and the Golden Dawn. The theosophists sought truth in the occult wisdom of the East, encompassing reincarnation, karma (the evolution of the soul), vegetarianism, astrology, transcendental meditation, and generally, all the mystical and occult arts.

Since Darwinism ruled scientific thought and man had been deprived of his basis for hope and faith, the latter part of the nineteenth century saw the quest for eternal life pursued through the ancient mysticisms and the practice of magic arts. These "spiritual" questers didn't stop with the rediscovery of ancient gnosticism. They were actively involved in the protection of animals and the new political movement of Fabian Socialism. The symbol of the Theosophical Society, founded in 1875, was a circle formed of a snake, with a swastika[6] enclosed in another circle at the top of the snake circle; this circle enclosed two interlocking triangles with an ankh (the symbol of the Egyptian god Ra) in the center. The society was founded by Helena Petrovna Blavatsky. Blavatsky claimed to have traveled throughout the Orient and central Asia, in particular Tibet. She claimed to have been initiated there into the secret mysteries of the universe. She also supposedly learned of the

Aryans,[7] who instructed the chosen in mystical knowledge. She espoused the existence of Lemuria, Hyperboreh, and Atlantis. Supposedly, the world's current races came from the Aryans, who had evolved from the bodiless entities of the Hyperboreans. Blavatsky said there were two more groups to come, and then we would begin the cycle again in another part of the universe. Darwin's evolution now had its "spiritual" counterpart in the "religious" sphere of man's life, a replacement for the Creator, the reborn ancient gnosticism. Some of Blavatsky's writings included *Isis Unveiled, The Voice of Silence,* and a magazine entitled *Lucifer.*

All of this mysticism bloomed in all its horror in Nazi Germany. All the evils of gnosticism, racial purity, pagan symbols, the quest for ancient "relics," mystic knowledge, and the occult brought a twelve-year rule of what can be justifiably called complete evil. The genesis of Nazism was in the Thule Society, founded in 1918 by Baron von Sebottendorf. He acknowledged gnostic guidance from the Egyptian mysteries of religious orders. Under him, racial purity of Aryan ancestry was made pre-imminent. Potential members had to research and prove this purity for three generations. The symbolism and religion of the subsequent Nazis can be summed up in a speech given by Sebottendorf on November 9, 1918:

"I intend to commit the Thule *Gesellschaft* to this combat, as long as I shall hold the Iron Hammer . . . I swear it on this swastika, on this sign which for us is sacred, in order that you hear it, O triumphant Sun! And I shall keep my faith with you. Have confidence in me as I have confidence in you . . . Our God is the father of battle and his rune is that of the eagle . . . which is the symbol of the Aryans. And to call attention to the fiery nature of the eagle, he will be shown in red eagle who reminds us that we must pass through death in order to live again."[8]

Earlier, Ernst Haeckel had embraced social Darwinism and the humanism of Marx. The evolution theories of biology, coupled with Marx's theories of economic evolution, were the justification, without guilt, for racial genocide. Those who did not represent the Aryan ideal of perfection or who were "parasites" upon humanity could be destroyed with impunity. Haeckel stated that "Politics is applied biology." These beliefs took root in Adolph Hitler. They were further reinforced by such books as *Moral and Intellectual Inequality of the Races* by Gobineau, a Frenchman who favored

Germany and German superiority. Goethe was still another influence, as were the operatic works of Richard Wagner. The Wagnerian symbols of the Grail and illumination, or enlightenment, as illustrated in *Parsifal;* ascetic purity; and mysticism all merged with tales of the Norse gods. Out of these tales and beliefs, the foundation of Nazism were laid down and made to appear good and "righteous."

In the early 1900s, Jorg Lanz von Liebenfels began publishing the magazine *Ostara*. It, too, promulgated the supremacy of the Aryan race, exemplified by blue eyes and blond hair. The doctrine of *Ostara* and the Thule Society merged. There were missions conducted to Montsegur in the Pyrenees, the last stronghold of the Cathars, to seek the Holy Grail. These were conducted by members of the Thule Society and later by the Nazis, the last occurring in 1944. They sought the Grail for occult purposes. Legends say that when Lucifer was cast out of Heaven, an emerald fell from his crown to earth. It was cut like a vase with 144 facets, and the Grail was created from it. It is interesting to note gnosticism's preoccupation with light, since Lucifer means "light-bearing angel." Gems are an integral part of gnosticism, and the emerald is considered the stone of prophecy.

The myths, legends, and esoteric knowledge, astrology, symbolism, and the spectacles of light at Nuremburg ensnared a people into the great travesty of the Third Reich. The SS was the equivalent of the "illuminati," or enlightened ones, while Hitler was the "master." In *The Occult and the Third Reich*, Jean-Michel Angebert writes that in 1939 Marcel Ray realized "the confrontation not far off, it will be a Manichean war or in the words of Scripture, a battle of the gods."[9] It was a battle to wipe this evil from the face of the earth. That it was evil has not been nor can it ever be denied. Was the evil destroyed? No. It just changed its garments and adapted to new conditions. Its companion movement, secular humanism, was growing well in the world and in the United States, specifically, all in the name of goodness and human compassion.

Today we call it "New Age," but it is not new. Today people search for meaning, inner light, personal growth, control of selves, self-knowledge, the principle of mind over matter, and unity with the universal consciousness. The war for men's minds and souls is again engaged with symbols, imagined light, and self-knowledge. We look to political leaders or gurus to save us and protect us, and they will not and cannot.

The scriptures tell us to test all spirits in John I, 4:1: "Beloved, believe not every spirit, but try the spirits whether they are of God: because many false prophets are gone out into this world."

Just because something presents itself as good and worthwhile does not make it truthful or right, else there would not be so many wrongful deeds in this world. Do not believe what any man says on the face of it. Test it; read and study the Word. It is your only source of truth in a world of lies. Discard the search for universal consciousness, cosmos connections, the astral planes, harmonics of the soul, rituals, and prognostication. Be wary of those who will "guide" you to a knowledge of self or reveal "secrets" to you. Do not place your faith in esoteric doctrines and practices. Do not be deluded by the false light of the imitator, Satan. Remember the true Light, described in John 1:4-13:

> In him was life; and the life was the light of men. And the light shineth in darkness; and the darkness comprehended it not. There was a man sent from God, whose name was John. The same came for a witness, to bear witness of the Light, that all men through him might believe. He was not that Light, but was sent to bear witness of that Light. That was the true Light, which lighteth every man that cometh into the world. He was in the world, and the world was made by him, and the world knew him not. He came unto his own, and his own received him not. But as many as received him, to them gave he power to become the sons of God, even to them that believe on his name: Which were born, not of blood, nor of the will of the flesh, nor of the will of man, but of God.

To do full justice to the gnostic beliefs, volumes would have to be written. Its weaving in and out of the history of mankind attests to its tenacity. What I have offered here can only serve as an introductory examination. It is hoped, however, that it will give you some new insights and assist you in recognizing gnosticism in its many guises, such as the earth spirits, or "mother earth." The wisdom of the Bible, not the vain imaginings of man, is the truth.

CHAPTER SEVEN

Education, Socialism, and Secular Humanism

Judeo-Christian principles formed the cornerstone in the building of our nation. Schools were created so that children could learn to read, chiefly to give them access to the scriptures, for it was generally held that from the Word came knowledge to live a happy, harmonious life. It was known that the Bible taught wisdom and strengthend the character so that one was not buffeted by every philosophy that might encroach upon the laws, both natural and spiritual, of God. Why, then, in this day of increasing knowledge, has spirituality become a hiss and a byword in education? Why, in a time of quantum leaps in the level of knowledge, have we forsaken wisdom?

Proverbs 1:3-7 tells us, "To receive the instruction of wisdom, justice, and judgment, and equity; To give subtly to the simple, to the young man knowledge and discretion. A wise man will hear, and will increase learning; and a man of understanding shall attain unto wise counsels: To understand a proverb, and the interpretation; the words of the wise, and their dark sayings. The fear of the Lord is the beginning of knowledge: but fools despise wisdom and instruction."

Have we become fools? Do we think that we can teach right and wrong without absolutes? Many schools, colleges, and universities are offering courses in "ethics," described as courses in moral conduct and behavior. These courses focus on our societal interactions, at both personal and business levels. This is traditionally the domain of religion. But these classes are called "ethics" because religion has become a shameful word in education.

Why are so many terrified of that simple little word, "religion"? Because religion recognizes the Creator, and to recognize His existence is very threatening. In doing so, man is forced to accept that he is not God; that he is not the giver of all good things, that he is not the source of law, and that in him there is no power but by God; not even the power to have life. Romans 1:28 puts it very plainly: "And even as they did not like to retain God in their knowledge, God gave them over to a reprobate mind, to do those things which are not convenient."

The schools of the United States are ignoring the source of law, knowledge, and wisdom. How can we teach decent living, respect for life and property, or what is euphemistically called "ethics" while denying the source? All manmade law is relative and changeable. Only the laws of God are absolute. They are the only laws upon which the foundation of a moral society can be built. Whether the citizens of other nations accept God or not, their laws governing the affairs of men are still based on these natural laws. The laws are not burdensome but, when followed, rather free us to live at peace with all men. They protect us and secure us.

One of our former strengths, our educational system, is being destroyed. Not all the money in the world, not all the books, nor computers, nor teachers can save it. The safety and security of law and order have been removed, exchanged for moral relativism and secular humanism, and therefore, chaos.

In removing the Ten Commandments and prayer from the schools, the government has removed peace, security, justice, discipline, trust, and refuge; and has replaced them with violence, lawlessness, inequity, chaos, deceit, and vulnerability. All things are made relative, changeable, and unstable. Ultimately, fear and insecurity rule the day.

The Ten Commandments are God's law for the believer, but the principles apply to the non-believer as well. Does a non-believer approve of lying, stealing, adultery, murder, jealousy, and disrespect of family? Hindus, Muslims, Buddhists, Jews, Christians, and atheists all agree that the commandments teach virtuous qualities. They can't be engendered, however, without acknowledging the source of virtue. There are two options: man or God. If we choose man, these qualities are rendered null and void by the very weakness of man himself, because his laws are so inconsistent and changing. These laws lack final authority. God's laws are constant and absolute, unchanging and eternal. God is the same yesterday, today and tomorrow. Christ did not change the Law; He fulfilled the Law. He said, Matthew 5:17-18, "Think not that I am come to destroy the law, or the prophets: I am not come to destroy, but to fulfil. For verily I say unto you, Till heaven and earth pass, one jot or one tittle shall in no wise pass from the law, till all be fulfilled."

The bottom line is that no agency of man, institution of man, no government of man, no educational institution, can stand without law and regulations founded on absolutes, and all Law emanates from Him, whether temporal or sacred. Any alteration of, tampering with, or perversion of the Law results in destruction. It may be slow in coming, but the erosion continues at a constantly accelerating pace until the inevitable collapse.

In the November 1992 issue of *Reader's Digest*, in an article by Eugene H. Methvin, the results of a poll on prayer were published. They were amazing, uplifting, and a reason for hope. Here are the results: "Do you approve or disapprove of the U.S. Supreme Court ruling that it is unconstitutional for a prayer to be offered at a high school graduation?" Eighty percent disapproved, and only 18 percent approved. "Do you generally favor or oppose prayer in public schools?" Seventy-five percent were in favor, and 19 percent disapproved. "Is it right for a school to display a manger scene or menorah during the holiday season?" Seventy-six percent agreed, and 21 percent disagreed. "Would you be more likely to vote for a candidate for President or Congress who favored prayer in the public schools?" Fifty-nine percent said they would be more likely to vote for this candidate, and only 16 percent said they would be less likely to do so.

These results are alarming in view of Supreme Court decisions. The vast majority of the citizens of these United States are inclined to value religion and want the recognition of God in schools. The parents are required to send their children to school each day by constraint of civil law, and yet the majority of parents are not permitted their wishes regarding something so dear—something that is guaranteed in the First Amendment of the Constitution. This guarantee is that government can "make no law respecting an establishment of religion or *prohibiting the free expression thereof.*" Maybe the Congress cannot prohibit, but the Supreme Court, by their rulings, certainly have. This debate has been going on since 1962. We do have redress, a means of righting a wrong. If the Supreme Court will not hearken to the original intentions of the Founding Fathers, then we must insist that our duly elected representatives act to correct this error. The Congress (both houses) have prayers at the opening of each day. They hold prayer breakfasts. The Supreme Court even invokes God.

Are our legislators a special, privileged, and elect group in the eyes of God? Their right to prayers seems to indicate that they are worthy of religious guidance and God's support, while our children are not. Children need spiritual guidance. They must be shown that there is meaning and goodness in this world. They are our future, and if they don't have this right, this freedom, this guarantee, soon, the future won't be worth having.

To teach our children morality, we need a yardstick, a measure against which all virtue is judged: The Law of God. It would appear that the "wisdom of man" prefers metal detectors, security guards, sex education, condoms, and abortion counseling. Would just five minutes a day, spent in the study of true morality and a moment of prayer, be foolish? No. The seeds of truth, mercy, and kindness, and a love of virtue would be born. These are the things of enduring value; the values that go into the inner man and go with him from the school to the street to his home and back again. Yes, we have an obligation to learn to use our talents to the best of our abilities, for they serve us, our community, and our nation, and this in turn serves God. We should strive to be the best that we can be, to work and to achieve.

The home is part of education, the most important part. We parents must teach the virtues in our daily lives. As Deuteronomy 11:18-20 teaches, "Therefore shall ye lay up these my words in your heart and in your soul, and bind them for a sign upon your hand, that they may be as frontlets between your eyes. And ye shall teach them your children, speaking of them when thou sittest in thine house, and when thou walkest by the way, when thou liest down, and when thou risest up. And thou shalt write them upon the door posts of thine house, and upon they gates." We are our children's first teachers.

We need to encourage our children in their studies, help when possible, but not take over. We must always find something to praise, no matter how small. We must let them stumble, too. How else will they learn to pick themselves up? We must give them space to struggle so that they will learn to walk tall, taking pride in conquering problems. We must teach them self-mastery, so that external forces don't bring them under compulsion. We must not only love them, but let them know that we do. We must also bring order and rules to their lives, as Proverbs 22:6 implies: "Train up a child in the way he should go: and when he is old, he will not depart from it."

Were our government-sponsored schools always so inept at teaching? Were they always the hotbeds of disorderly conduct and disrespect that we see constantly on television or read about in the papers? Were they always graduating students who were functionally illiterate? No. What has happened, then? Please notice that I called our schools "government schools," not public schools. Yes, they are supported by public funds, our taxes, but they are not run by the public at large; rather, they are controlled by bureaucratic spokesmen and social experimenters. They try this and then they try that, and when this and that don't work, they move on to some other fad. Our children and our nation are the victims of these theoretical approaches to education.

When the early colonists came to this continent and settled in this land, they came pursuing spiritual and secular freedom with a recognition of the importance of education to both aspects of their lives. Because reading was important and the only avenue to know the laws of God, education was imperative. Mothers taught their children, and the Bible was, of course, the principal text. Later, private schools and tuition-free schools for the public supported by philanthropy served to educate the children. Benjamin Harris introduced America's first textbook, *The New England Primer*, in 1790. In the preface to his 1991 reprint of Harris's primer, David Barton explains that this textbook "was the beginning text for students; until 1900 it continued to be a principal text in all types of American schools." What was in this wonderful little book? Opening with "A Divine Song of Praise to God for a Child," the book contained the alphabet, a rhyming alphabet based on the scriptures—for example, "Young pious Ruth, Left all for Truth." The book is full of questions, answers, and prayers taken from scripture. There is even an alphabet of "Lessons for Youth." For the letter "B" the lesson is, "Better is a little with the fear of the Lord than great treasure and trouble therewith." Those in charge of schooling did not separate absolutes nor God from our educational bodies.

Historically, moral education was considered to be a prerequisite for the duties of citizenship in our young nation. At the time of our nation's establishment in the eighteenth century, schooling took place in the home, at churches, at private academies, and sometimes in supported schools for those in need of public help. State control (government schools) was nonexistent and not anticipated. Our founding fathers equated education with religion. The two went hand in hand, for surely one supported the other. The schools of the townships were never intended to supersede parents; but rather to aid them in fulfilling their scriptural obligations to their children, as defined in Deuteronomy 6:4-7: "Hear, O Israel: The Lord our God is one Lord: And thou shalt love the Lord thy God with all thine heart, and with all thy soul, and with all thy might. And these words, which I command thee this day, shall be in thine heart: And thou shalt teach them diligently unto thy children, and shalt talk of them when thou sittest in thine house, and when thou walkest by the way, and when thou liest down, and when thou risest up."

Parents under the authority of God must feed, clothe, and *educate* their children. In 1784 the New Hampshire Constitution affirmed that "morality and piety, rightly grounded on evangelical principles, will give the greatest security to government." They provided public support of education.

The Massachusetts Constitution of 1780 stated that education was to be given to the people because it was "necessary for the preservation of their rights and liberties." This education was to include schooling for "Wisdom and knowledge, as well as virtue." Gradually, tax-supported schools began to take shape in each of the new states. In Virginia, Thomas Jefferson was one of the leading champions of schooling by tax-supported institutions. Those in the upper class attended private schools. Finally, in 1829, schools for the poor were made mandatory. These were the beginnings of government schools as we have come to know them today.

Alexis de Tocqueville said, "I sought for the greatness and genius of America in her commodious harbors and her ample rivers—and it was not there.... in her fertile fields and boundless forests—and it was not there....in her rich mines and her vast world commerce—and it was not there....in her democratic Congress and her matchless Constitution—and it was not there. Not until I went into the churches of America and heard her pulpits flame with righteousness did I understand the secret of her genius and power: America is great because she is good, and if America ever ceases to be good, America will cease to be great."[1]

De Tocqueville saw then what we fail to see around us now. The schools of those times were a reflection and extension of a national mind set, inclined toward virtue and absolutes with a love of good and God.

Are the public schools of today the same as yesterday? Is their purpose the same? Are they in existence to teach "Wisdom, knowledge and virtue"? The seeming goal of today's schools is knowledge. Where is wisdom? Where is virtue? Where are values? Today bureaucrats, supported by misguided judiciary, say we cannot teach values because they are discriminatory or cause intolerance.

In his book *The Closing of the American Mind*, Dr. Allan Bloom speaks of the "Founders" giving us an open society which was "to provide a respectable place" for "minorities—to wrest respect from those who were not disposed to give it—and to weaken the sense of superiority of the dominant majority . . . That dominant majority gave the country a dominant culture with its traditions, its literature, its tastes, its special claim to know and supervise the language and its Protestant religions"—"Much of the intellectual machinery of twentieth century American political thought and social science was constructed for the purposes of making an assault on that majority."[2] He goes on to say that the Founders were striving for a "national majority concerning the fundamental rights and then prevent that majority from using its power to overturn those fundamental rights."

In Franklin, Massachusetts, on May 4, 1796, Horace Mann was born in poverty. Depending on his own initiative, with the aid of a few teachers and the use of the Franklin town library, he educated himself and finally gained admittance to Brown University, where he was the valedictorian of his graduating class in 1819. Later, he studied at Litchfield Law School and was admitted to the bar in 1823. He served in the state house of representatives and later as president of the Massachusetts Senate. Because of his difficulties in obtaining an education, he established a state board of education and gave up his political career to become its first secretary in 1837. He served in this post for eleven years, earning the title, "Father of American Public Education."

Horace Mann believed the following educational principles:
1. For freedom in the Republic to be lasting, children must be educated
2. Public schools should be supported by taxation of the citizens
3. All students should be accepted regardless of religion, economic status, or ethnicity
4. No religious group should exert special influence
5. Only professionally trained teachers should be employed.

I believe that Mann took certain characteristics for granted, assuming they would remain in place. In his first principle, he assumed that citizens would always understand the price at which their freedom had been purchased, and why. In his second principle, he believed that the public will would not be supplanted by special interests or the judiciary. In his fourth principle, Mann removed specific doctrine of denominations and sects from the schools, which has led us to remove all teachings on virtue from public education. In the fifth principle, it is noted that he was dependent on the internal self-discipline of a people living in a free society. Little did Mann realize that the virtues and internal discipline instilled by the teaching of virtues would disappear in the public school systems that he so dearly loved and promulgated. He did not live to see God and moral education stripped away from his greatest achievement. He never faced the fact that he took from parents their greatest obligation and right and instead gave children over to the power of the state. In his noble intentions, he did not recognize that the institutions of men lay open for the subverting and perverting of truth and thereby paved the way for the destruction of the very thing he sought to preserve through education—a free society of men.

John Locke explains the parental responsibility: "Adam and Eve, and after them all parents were, by the Law of Nature, under an obligation to preserve, nourish, and educate the children they had begotten, not as their own workmanship, but the workmanship of their own Maker, the Almighty, to whom they were accountable for them."[3]

Parents no longer have complete authority to mold, instruct, and shape their children's minds in matters of religion, morality, and freedom. In the name of the "common good," the state has gradually usurped this right and obligation while parents, to a large extent, have abrogated their privileges to the state.

In a speech documenting the demise of our educational system before the House of Representatives on March 21, 1952, Representative Ron Shafer, from the state of Michigan, made the following statement, which is copied from the Congressional Record.

> Certain basic premises characterize this movement:
>
> First, it proclaims that capitalism in the United States is doomed—that it is dead, or dying—and that its replacement by some form of collectivism, by some form or degree of planned economy, government control, or outright socialization, essentially new and different in character, is both desirable and inevitable.
>
> Second, this movement and its sponsors hold that the schools should participate actively in building a new social order along these collectivist lines, that this activity should be carried on either through outright indoctrination of these premises and concepts or through processes of guided group study and discussion and uncoerced persuasion within the classroom, and that the schools, through both the content and methods of instruction, should prepare and condition the child for participation in that new social order.
>
> Third, the movement calls for such revision of the educational system, and of its philosophy, procedures, and subject matter, as is necessary to advance and accomplish these purposes.
>
> Fourth, more extreme educational sponsors of this movement also hold that the transition to collectivism will, in all probability, involve class conflict; that the schools, accordingly, should adopt the class approach in their educational activities, align themselves with the worker class, and utilize class consciousness and conflict as a "potential resource."
>
> Fifth, advocates of the program of social reconstruction through

the schools recognize the inevitability of opposition to that program and accordingly propose certain "steps to power" designed to enable the schools and the profession to deal, both offensively and defensively, with the anticipated resistance.

Sixth, the movement also includes advocacy of a variety of other subsidiary proposals for changes in the form, philosophy, and procedures of government in the United States.

Seventh, since teachers are envisioned by this movement as "engineers of social change," the political-economic-social views of teachers become a matter of vital concern to advocates of social reconstruction through the schools.

Eighth, since the Second World War, the program of social reconstruction through the schools has received significant restatement in a formally adopted program of the progressive education organization.

Ninth, a further postwar development in the movement has been the addition of the goal of world government and a supernational sovereignty to the program of social reconstruction through the schools.

These are the main features, the principal tenets, of the movement here being described, and the foregoing summary constitutes a brief outline of the material documented herein.

Before the decline outlined in Representative Shafer's statement, public schools had a great deal to contribute to the common good of our nation. They emphasized seeking and discovering truths, allowed for discrimination against lies and deceit, and upheld the rights to opinions based on these discoveries. Education was intended to develop in children the tools for seeking knowledge and wisdom, and to strengthen the conscience, so that virtue would guide them to use knowledge and wisdom well. This is a model that still applies today: Schools should instruct students in those disciplines that will guide them in their pursuits—namely, reading, spelling, grammar and mathematics; and those skills should be coupled with virtue, initiative, and curiosity. These are the keys to all the gates of learning. Without them, progress will be stifled. Today's schools seem more interested in social engineering than in education and far more interested in "political correctness" than in the pursuit of truth. They stifle curiosity, there are no absolutes, no truth, no need to study. The question is why? What happened? Why did these bastions for good become a blight upon our moral and political lives?

"If you plan for a year, plant a seed. If for ten years, plant a tree. If for a hundred years, teach the people. When you sow a seed once, you will reap a single harvest. When you teach the people, you will reap a hundred harvests," said Kuan Chung Kuan. The Intercollegiate Socialist Society understood this principle very well. The founders of this group were Upton Sinclair, Jack London, Thomas Wentworth Higginson (first president), J. G. Phelps Stokes, and Clarence Darrow.[4] The birth of the Intercollegiate Socialist Society (ISS) was on September 12, 1905, at Peck's Restaurant on Fulton Street in New York City. The purpose was "to promote an intelligent interest in Socialism among college men and women." They later established the headquarters at the Rand School of Social Science in 1908. Soon, chapters were organized in leading universities such as Harvard, University of Wisconsin, Barnard, and Wayne. Such notables as Walter Lippman, Walter Reuther, and Eugene V. Debs were either chapter presidents or active members of the group![5]

The movement flourished and by 1917 had chapters in "61 schools of higher learning and in a dozen graduate bodies," as stated by John Howland Snow in his book *The Turning of the Tides*.[6] Snow explains in great detail the influence of Fabian Societies of Great Britain, which were guided by people such as George Bernard Shaw and H. G. Wells; their goal was socialism. The British Fabian Society's Forty-ninth Annual Report stated, "we continue active association—with the League for Industrial Democracy of New York which carries on active propaganda in the United States on very similar lines to our own work here—."

In 1945 one of the Fabian Society's members, Clement Attlee, became prime minister of England. Ellen Wilkinson became minister of education under Attlee. She was a former member of the Communist Party and resigned upon her election to Parliament on the Labor Ticket in 1924. For years she was on the executive council of the Fabian Society and lectured in American cities under the auspices of the League for Industrial Democracy.[7]

The League for Industrial Democracy was the former Intercollegiate Socialist Society, renamed in 1921. Its primary purpose was "education for a new social order based on production for use and not for profit." All the former chapters were united into LID, and in the 1930s, John Dewey, the "progressive educator," was its vice-president. In 1941 Dewey, who had founded the American Association of University Professors in 1915, became its president. In 1919 the Progressive Education Association was formed to further the philosophy of "progressive" education expounded by Mr. Dewey. Traditional subjects and methods were altered with the intention of turning the schools into social laboratories of learning by which the society would be molded according to certain social values. With the socialists' minds bent on collectivism and destruction of traditional values at the forefront, it is no wonder that schools have been on a downward spiral.

The socialists started by recruiting fresh and impressionable college minds in the early 1900s, then those idealistic (and deluded) young teachers moved into American classrooms, and gradually the traditional virtues of the founders of this nation were twisted. Absolutes were rejected, the search for truth submerged, and "freedom" was advocated, with no guidelines or constraints. The circle of involvement in this philosophy enlarged from generation to generation, its adherents constantly multiplying, with the result that aside from a few carefully safeguarded schools, socialism is the nationally accepted policy and philosophy of schooling and education, hiding under the term "progressive." The irony is that this movement is just the opposite; it is regressive. If we are not motivated to act quickly, the inevitable results will not only be classroom anarchy, which is evidenced by the number of teachers leaving the classrooms because of the lack of discipline, but finally civil anarchy, giving rise to the need for externally imposed discipline upon the nation by civil authority to restore order. True democracy, as we have known it, could cease to exist. True freedom can only exist when there are limits placed upon a man by himself, limits that are an extension of his reason through an understanding and appreciation of absolutes. Those virtues can only be understood by the light of the Word of God. Our public schools have denied our most basic educational necessity, instruction in morality and virtue.

This travesty is supported under the principle of separation of church and state. But religion was not removed from the schools; instead, Judeo-Christian teachings were replaced with the new religion of secular humanism. It must be remembered that in addition to leadership in the ISS and the LID, Mr. Dewey was a signer of the Humanist Manifesto. What is humanism? The dictionary defines it as "any system of thought based on the interests and ideals of man." The manifesto itself states, "Humanism is faith in the supreme value and self-perfectibility of human personality." The manifesto's authors didn't stop here but went further, saying, "Religious humanists regard the universe as self-existing and not created—as non-theists, we begin with humans, not God, nature, not deity. . . . But we can discover no divine purpose or providence for the human species. While there is much we do not know, humans are responsible for what we are or will become. No deity will save us; we must save ourselves." Humanism, then, was announced as a faith and religion, with man as the object of veneration. Religion has not been separated from the public school. It is alive and well, and it is idolatrous, the created rather than the Creator being the object of devotion. Since each man, according to the manifesto, was his own "god," all final and absolute and authority was removed, being vested now in each individual.

Mr. Dewey, in his *Quest for Certainty,* published in 1929, said, "Judgements about values are judgements about the conditions and the results of experienced objects: judgements about that which should regulate the formation of our desires, affections, and enjoyments." Simply put, the philosophy is: If it feels good and works for you, do it, and if it causes you pain and doesn't work for you, don't do it. This philosophy has major repercussions for society. Children no longer need to respect parents; husbands and wives don't need to be faithful to each other; abortion is acceptable. Even sexual perversion, rape, drug use, looting, and any other abominable behavior would, by extension, be acceptable. Each individual becomes a law unto himself. One could object that civil law moderates and codifies the interactions of society. Not so, for if the final authority of truth is destroyed, no law of mankind has any moral authority, and consequently there is no need for obedience to it, faith in it, or respect for it. The only result of humanism is anarchy and chaos, for all law has broken down and there is no place of security or refuge, whether it be home, school, workplace, courtroom, or even the physical church.

The new religion of secular humanism has left man destitute of protection physically and spiritually. Out of the phrase "judgements about conditions and the results of experienced objects," we have "situation ethics," so that a Charles Keating or a Michael Milken may be justified. Congressmen no longer have to be concerned about check kiting or overdrafts. Rioting in large cities becomes not only acceptable but understandable and is regarded as a legitimate response to "experience." In its extreme, humanism would justify Adolph Hitler, Joseph Stalin, or sanction any despotic act. The ramifications of this manmade religion are so far-reaching that its evil is permeating every fiber of our society. This is the major philosophy of the school systems. Everyone, public and government, wants to "fix and repair" our education system. Restore absolutes; restore the moral authority of law and virtue; restore the Ten Commandments; restore the Creator to His creations, and you will restore an orderly society, protection of the individual and his property, and respect for civil authority and the right rule of law.

President Abraham Lincoln's proclamation of a National Fast Day, March 30, 1863, said:

> We have been the recipients of the choicest bounties of Heaven. We have been preserved, these many years, in peace and prosperity. We have grown in numbers, wealth and power, as no other nation has ever grown. But we have forgotten God. We have forgotten the gracious hand which preserved us in peace, and multiplied and enriched and strengthened us; and we have vainly imagined, in the deceitfulness of our hearts, that all these blessings were produced by some superior wisdom and virtue of our own. Intoxicated with unbroken success, we have become too self-sufficient to feel the necessity of redeeming and preserving grace, too proud to pray to the God that made us.[8]

What Lincoln so aptly perceived in his day has only grown stronger with time.

Although the cause of public education is noble, it is fraught with problems. The secularizing of the public schools begun by Horace Mann in the 1830s was brought to completion by the United States Supreme Court in the October 1962 term in the *Abington School District v. Schempp* case. The decision was rendered on June 17, 1963.

School District of Abington Township, Pennsylvania, et al. v. Schempp et al. Because of the prohibition of the First Amendment against the enactment by Congress of any law "respecting an establishment of religion," which is made applicable to the States by the Fourteenth Amendment, no state law or school board may require that passages from the Bible be read or that the Lord's Prayer be recited in the public schools of a State at the beginning of each school day—even if the individual students may be excused from attending or participating in such exercises upon written request of their parents.

Mr. Justice Clark delivered the opinion of the Court:

Once again we are called upon to consider the scope of the provision of the First Amendment to the United States Constitution, which declares that "Congress shall make no law respecting an establishment of religion, or prohibiting free exercise thereof . . ." These companion cases present the issues in the context of state action requiring that schools begin each day with readings from the Bible. While raising the basic questions under slightly different factual situations, the cases permit of joint treatment. In light of the history of the First Amendment and of our cases interpreting and applying its requirements, we hold that the practices at issue and the laws requiring them are unconstitutional under the Establishment Clause, as applied to the states through the Fourteenth Amendment.

The petition particularized the petitioners' atheistic beliefs and stated that the rule, as practiced, violated their rights:

in that it threatens their religious liberty by placing a premium on belief as against non-belief and subjects their freedom of conscience to the rule of the majority; it pronounces belief in God as the source of all moral and spiritual values, equating these values with religious values, and thereby renders sinister, alien and suspect the beliefs and ideals of your Petitioners, promoting doubt and question of their morality, good citizenship and good faith.

In *Zorach v. Clauson*, 343 U.S. 306, 313 (1952), we gave specific recognition to the proposition that "we are a religious people whose institutions presuppose a Supreme Being.

This is not to say, however, that religion has been so identified with our history and government that religious freedom is not likewise as strongly imbedded in our public and private life.

Almost a hundred years ago in *Minor v. Board of Education of Cincinnati,* Judge Alphonso Taft, father of the revered chief justice, in an unpublished opinion, stated the ideal of our people regarding religious freedom as one of "absolute equality before the law, of all religious opinions and sects . . . ." Mr. Justice Stewart, dissenting, said:

> I think the records in the two cases before us are so fundamentally deficient as to make impossible an informed or responsible determination of the constitutional issues presented. Specifically, I cannot agree that on these records we can say that the Establishment Clause has necessarily been violated. But I think there exist serious questions under both that provision and the Free Exercise Clause—insofar as each is imbedded in the Fourteenth Amendment—which require the remand of these cases for the taking of additional evidence.
>
> The First Amendment declares that "Congress shall make no law respecting an establishment of religion, or prohibiting the free exercise thereof . . . ." It is, I think, a fallacious oversimplification to regard these two provisions as establishing a single constitutional standard of "separation of church and state," which can be mechanically applied in every case to delineate the required boundaries between government and religion. We err in the first place if we do not recognize, as a matter of history and as a matter of the imperatives of our free society, that religion and government must necessarily interact in countless ways. Secondly, the fact is that while in many contexts the Establishment Clause and the Free Exercise Clause fully complement each other, there are areas in which a doctrinaire reading of the Establishment Clause leads to irreconcilable conflict with the Free Exercise Clause.
>
> A single obvious example should suffice to make the point. Spending federal funds to employ chaplains for the armed forces might be said to violate the Establishment Clause. Yet a lonely soldier stationed at some faraway outpost could surely complain that a government which did *not* provide him the opportunity for pastoral guidance was affirmatively prohibiting the free exercise of his religion. And such examples could readily be multiplied. The short of the matter is simply that the two relevant clauses of the First

Amendment cannot accurately be reflected in a sterile metaphor which by its very nature may distort rather than illumine the problems involved in a particular case. Sherbert v. Verner, Post, p. 398.

As a matter of history, the First Amendment was adopted solely as a limitation upon the newly created National Government. The events leading to its adoption strongly suggest that the Establishment Clause was primarily an attempt to insure that Congress not only would be powerless to establish a national church, but would also be unable to interfere with existing state establishments. See McGowan v. Maryland, 366 U.S. 420, 440-441. Each State was left free to go its own way and pursue its own policy with respect to religion. Thus Virginia from the beginning pursued a policy of disestablishmentarianism. Massachusetts, by contrast, had an established church until well into the nineteenth century.

So matters stood until the adoption of the Fourteenth Amendment, or more accurately, until this Court's decision in Cantwell v. Connecticut, in 1940. 310 U.S. 296. In that case the Court said: "The First Amendment declares that Congress shall make no law respecting an establishment of religion or prohibiting the free exercise thereof. The Fourteenth Amendment has rendered the legislatures of the states as incompetent as Congress to enact such laws.

But I cannot agree with what seems to me the insensitive definition of the Establishment Clause contained in the Court's opinion, nor with the different but, I think, equally mechanistic definition contained in the separate opinions which have been filed.

And in Cantwell v. Connecticut, supra, the purpose of those guarantees was described in the following terms: "On the one hand, it forestalls compulsion by law of the acceptance of any creed or the practice of any form of worship. Freedom of conscience and freedom to adhere to such religious organization or form of worship as the individual may choose cannot be restricted by law. On the other hand, it safeguards the free exercise of the chosen religion." 310 U.S., at 303.

It is this concept of constitutional protection embodied in our decisions which makes the cases before us such difficult ones for me. For there is involved in these cases a substantial free exercise claim on the part of those who affirmatively desire to have their children's school day open with the reading of passages from the Bible.

It might be argued that parents who want their children exposed to religious influences can adequately fulfill that wish off school property and outside school time. With all its surface persuasiveness, however, this argument seriously misconceives the basic constitutional justification for permitting the exercises at issue in these cases. For a *compulsory state educational system* so structures a child's life that if religious exercises are held to be an impermissible activity in schools, *religion is placed at an artificial and state-created disadvantage.* Viewed in this light, permission of such exercises for those who want them is necessary if the schools are truly to be neutral in the matter of religion. *And a refusal to permit religious exercises thus is seen, not as the realization of state neutrality, but rather as the establishment of a religion of secularism,* or at least, as government support of the beliefs of those who think that religious exercises should be conducted only in private.

What our Constitution indispensably protects is the freedom of each of us, be he Jew or Agnostic, Christian or Atheist, Buddhist or Freethinker, to believe or disbelieve, to worship or not to worship, to pray or keep silent, according to his own conscience, uncoerced and unrestrained by government. It is conceivable that these school boards, or even all school boards, might eventually find it impossible to administer a system of religious exercises during school hours in such a way as to meet this constitutional standard—in such a way as completely to free from any kind of official coercion those who do not affirmatively want to participate. But I think we must not assume that school boards so lack the qualities of inventiveness and good will as to make impossible the achievement of that goal.

I would remand both cases for further hearings.[9]

Can the dilemma we are facing be put any more clearly?

CHAPTER EIGHT

The Responsibilities of Citizenship

If you are a Christian, your spiritual duty has been described for you:

> Ye are the salt of the earth: but if the salt have lost his savour, wherewith shall it be salted? it is thenceforth good for nothing, but to be cast out, and to be trodden under foot of men. Ye are the light of the world. A city that is set on a hill cannot be hid. Neither do men light a candle, and put it under a bushel, but on a candlestick; and it giveth light unto all that are in the house. Let your light so shine before men that they may see your good works, and glorify your Father which is in heaven (Matthew 5:13-16).

In a world that is morally corrupt and dark, God depends on Christians to be the "salt" and "light." That is our first duty. However, as members of society, we also have many civic duties. Christ told us in Matthew 22:21, "Render therefore unto Caesar the things which are Caesar's; and unto God the things that are God's"; that is, the material things of this world versus the spiritual. Just as we must be active spiritually, taxes must be paid and laws must be observed.

Mercifully, for more than two hundred years, the United States has offered a way of life that allows its citizens to fulfill their duties both to God and the state, in that order. As a result, our nation has been a bastion of religious freedom in the world. However, since the 1930s, this freedom has been increasingly threatened. In order to safeguard our nation's future, we must keep in mind the spirit in which our nation was formed.

Our forefathers were men of conviction, and such men do great things. They came to this country seeking freedom from religious persecution, freedom to worship their Creator, and freedom of self-determination. They were prepared to die for these freedoms, and if England had subdued the colonies, many of them undoubtedly would have died. Instead, the moral and spiritual strength of our forebears laid the foundation of our great nation.

The framers of our federal government, our greatest heroes and patriots, made it clear in the documents they wrote that their strength derived from faith in God. The First Amendment states, "Congress shall make no law respecting an establishment of religion, or prohibiting the free exercise thereof; or abridging the freedom of speech, or of the press; or the right of the people to peaceably assemble, and to petition the government for a redress of grievances."

According to the Constitution, then, our government cannot force us to worship in a specific way, nor should it prohibit us from worshipping. We are free to speak of our faith, free to write about it, free to attend worship assemblies. Never was such freedom known in this world until the birth of the United States of America. We must treasure this freedom, thank God for it, and above all work to preserve it. Our freedom does not exempt us from responsibilities; instead, our responsibilities are greater. That is the nature of a democracy.

One of our primary responsibilities as U.S. citizens is to vote responsibly. We should try to vote for men who exemplify high moral character, the virtues of which God approves and we can know from His Word. The Ten Commandments were the first laws that governed Christian men and women, and prepared them to receive the Christ on earth: "Wherefore the law was our schoolmaster to bring us unto Christ, that we might be justified by faith. But after that faith is come, we are no longer under a schoolmaster" (Galatians 3:24-25).

The Ten Commandments were not nullified by the coming of Jesus Christ; rather, his birth was a fulfillment of the commandments' power. These laws are still in force today. People who obey these laws are admired openly by many (and even secretly by others), and adherence to such fundamental principles is the least we should expect of our nation's leaders.

The commandments of the Mosaic Law tell us how to conduct ourselves, but the condition of men's hearts is also important: "For as he thinketh in his heart, so is he: Eat and drink, saith he to thee, but his heart is not with thee" (Proverbs 23:7).

Upright men are patient, sober-minded, slow to anger, industrious, just, vigilant, quick to listen, slow to speak, and stable in their words, deeds, and actions. They are not given to lying, double-mindedness, stealing, envy, vengeance, or false pride. These are qualities respected by people worldwide. Of course, these same qualities are often hated as well. How can these qualities be hated? Because it is not easy to manipulate people of high moral character; they aren't like reeds blown in the wind; they don't say yes or no and then do something else. Yes, they may compromise and negotiate in worldly affairs, but they don't compromise their principles, their honor, or their virtue. They don't change like Texas weather. Consistency is their hallmark.

It is not always easy to know whether a person is sincere. None of us can actually look into the heart of a man. We will never know his secret fears, his secret jealousies, or his secret angers. But there is much to be ascertained from his public conduct and the company he keeps. A person full of impatience cannot long conceal it. A liar will be found out. It is true that we can be deceived, so we must be watchful: "Be ye therefore wise as serpents, and harmless as doves" (Matthew 10:16). In other words, we should be vigilant, but without malice. We must carefully measure our candidates by the policies they advocate. If those policies are in opposition to the Scriptures, then we must not vote for them. We must seek men who best seem to meet high standards of conduct. Character is important. We must cut through all the political rhetoric and look at the character of the person who seeks our vote. For what does he stand? For what does his party stand? Who are the people around him? What is his record? What is his stance? Does he uphold morality? Does he accept responsibility?

We have the unique ability to choose our framers of national policy. We have the responsibility to choose wisely and carefully and be guided by the Word of God. We have been given much, and much will be expected of us in return:

> Submit yourselves to every ordinance of man for the Lord's sake: whether it be to the king as supreme; or unto governors, as unto them that are sent by him for the punishment of evildoers, and for the praise of them that do well. For so is the will of God, that with well doing ye may put to silence the ignorance of foolish men: As free, and not using your liberty for a cloak of maliciousness, but as the servants of God. Honour all men. Love the brotherhood. Fear God. Honour the king (1 Peter 2:13-17).

Our responsibilities to civil authority are well enumerated. This scripture presents a portrait of a good citizen of any state.

In secular matters, the civil law is the final word. We cannot be selective about which laws we will obey. We can, however, be selective regarding our leaders in the first place. If our leaders tax us, and pass laws about our daily behavior on a local, state, and national level, isn't it reasonable that we would not choose office-holders who will burden us with laws that may be contrary to the supreme law of God?

In the time of the Roman Empire, the Caesars were not only the political leaders of Rome, but its spiritual leaders as well, holding the title Papas Maximus. Temples in Rome, on its roads, and in cities all across the empire were ruled by Caesar. Yet Paul the Apostle was a citizen of Rome. And Christianity thrived there, because none could justly speak evil of the Christians; they were good citizens of the Empire. In fact, Paul writes of Roman Christians in Philippians 4:22, "All the saints salute you, chiefly they that are of Caesar's household."

It is an astounding fact that Christians were in some form of service to Caeser, that they were so trusted that they could be of service to men who were the total antithesis, spiritually, of everything in which they placed their faith. Obviously, the Christians did not rebel against Caeser's worldy authority. Instead, they proved themselves trustworthy, hard-working, and obedient. When the Caesars proclaimed themselves gods, only then did Christians rebel, but not in an overt manner. Only when called upon to bow down and worship the Caesars as gods did they refuse to obey the state. In civil matters, the state was obeyed; in spiritual matters, God was obeyed. (Years later, a group of Christians was falsely accused of burning Rome, and great suffering followed.) They did not hold "peaceful" marches or demonstrations, chain themselves to gates, or bring ridicule upon the name of Christ in any way; they led sober, diligent lives.

Their sobriety and diligence were a form of meekness, which is a quality the Scriptures ask us to cultivate: "Put them in mind to be subject to principalities and powers, to obey magistrates, to be ready to every good work, to speak evil of no man, to be no brawlers, but gentle, shewing all meekness unto all men" (Titus 3:1-2).

Unfortunately, meekness is often confused with weakness. The adjective "meek "comes from the Greek *praus* or *praos* and denotes gentleness and mildness in action. As a noun, meekness comes from the Greek word *prautes/praotes* and deals chiefly with a state of mind toward God, signifying a complete submission to His will. This submission gives man great power, because he then has access to the limitless help of God. Meekness can give man great resolve, security, and firmness. One can neither be weak nor proud, because true meekness of spirit negates both.

Since Christians were able to be good citizens under a tyrannical government, aren't we free to be even better citizens? Christians in the first century A.D. didn't have the right to vote, the power to choose their leaders, or even to leave their country if they didn't like it. I am afraid, at times, that modern Christians have had it too easy. We are so richly blessed to live in this republic. Let's not take it for granted. Our forefathers believed in divine help and sought it. We must do the same in order to protect the nation they fought to establish.

The foundation of our country was faith in God and His Word, and that faith continues to serve as the foundation of our lives. "If the foundations be destroyed, what can the righteous do?" This question, from Psalm 11:3, is also a warning. To say that how we vote doesn't matter is fallacious. If the German people had not followed Adolph Hitler, World War II might not have happened.

Another aspect of civic duty is work. God commanded man to work in Genesis 2:15: "And the lord God took the man and put him into the garden of Eden to dress it and to keep it." In Genesis 3:17, the work became hard: "And unto Adam he said, Because thou has harkened unto the voice of thy wife, and hast eaten of the tree, of which I commanded thee, saying, Thou shalt not eat of it: cursed is the ground for thy sake, in sorrow shalt thou eat of it all the days of thy life."

This obstacle helped man to flourish, however. Man had to set goals, to accomplish more, and against greater odds. We have inherited this strength, and work continues to shape us into better people. Work, instead of being demeaning, builds self-esteem. This is especially true in the United States, where we are free to choose our work, or change it if we dislike it. This freedom has made our nation prosperous, both because people are willing to work harder if they find their work worthwhile, and because innovation and talent are encouraged.

The subject of work seems naturally tied to that of money. Money, it should be noted, is not in conflict with leading a spiritual life. In fact, the wealthy people are able to help others, both through charity and through enterprises that provide work for other people. Instead of envying or even resenting the wealthy, we should be grateful to them. A poor man cannot give me a job; for that I must turn to the rich man, or to companies and corporations that have accumulated resources.

Prosperity is no sin. Look at Job, at Abraham and Solomon. They provided food, clothing, and shelter for many people. Because a man has wealth does not automatically mean that he is evil, any more than a poor man can be called virtuous simply because he is poor. Virtue does not reside in possessions or the absence of them. Be thankful that men prosper, because it is from them that we obtain jobs and honest labor. We should pray that they prosper, for in doing so we actually help ourselves. If they prosper, we have an opportunity to prosper through our intellect and our workmanship.

For a moment, imagine that there were no prosperous people. There would be no factories, no goods to buy. What would we do? This could not last. Man's nature to achieve would come to the forefront. Monetary equality, as envisioned under communism and socialism, has failed. Rejoice that you live in a land that, until recent times, has sought to keep men free in body, intellect and property.

Prosperity, though, can become a sin, when it is sought for its own sake. In this case, it becomes idolatry, and only the fool takes security in it.

In Luke 12:16-21, Christ told a parable about wealth:

> The ground of a certain rich man brought forth plentifully: And he thought within himself, saying, What shall I do, because I have no room where to bestow my fruits? And he said, This will I do: I will pull down my barns, and build greater; and there will I bestow all my fruits and my goods. And I will say to my soul, Soul, thou hast much goods laid up for many years; take thine ease, eat, drink, and be merry. But God said unto him, Thou fool, this night thy soul shall be required of thee: then whose shall those things be, which thou has provided? So is he that layeth up treasure for himself, and is not rich toward God.

We must not forget that it is our first and last duty to be rich toward God. In the United States, we consume "things" like no other people. We want designer clothes, bigger houses, faster cars, and so it goes. The more we have, the more we want. The worst part is that we have been deluded into the belief that the government can and should arrange for us to get whatever we want. Our elected officials have succeeded beyond all expectation in answering our demands. They have succeeded so well that our nation is $5 trillion in debt. Individuals are worried that they cannot pay their personal debts. We have bought into a big lie. We cannot spend our way into fiscal responsibility personally, and we cannot do it as a nation. We have a choice to make. If we want our elected representatives to act in a moral, disciplined, and responsible manner, then we must do the same. We must not rob or steal from future generations in the name of instant gratification. We must remember that temporary self-denial can bring great results. The young couple who spends and charges on their plastic to the limit will wind up paying only interest every month, with little hope of ever saving enough to make a down payment on a home.

My father, who was born in the very early 1900s, and who often wished in the 1930s that he had a nickel for a hamburger, never bought a house or car or anything on credit. He practiced a little self-denial, saved his money, and paid cash. He also never refused anyone who needed help. He was not rich, but he was rich in what mattered: family, friends, neighbors, and honor.

Like Paul, maybe we need to change our attitudes. Instead of asking what our government can do for us, we should ask what can we do for ourselves. As upright citizens, we can make better decisions for ourselves and our families than government can make for us collectively. The door was opened in the 1930s to creeping socialism. It was done with good intentions, but the results have proven troublesome to say the least. We are no longer the served. We are servants to a system that loves money, a system that believes money is the cure for every problem. The scriptures tells us that "the love of money is the root of all evil" (Timothy I, 6:10). Trusting in money, no matter who is spending it, will bring us to ruin. By exchanging need for want, we are turning money into an instrument of evil. As a nation, we should revitalize our moral principles and renew our work ethic, and stop saying, "Why doesn't the government do something?"

CHAPTER NINE

When Government Does Too Much

"Why doesn't the government do something?"
"The government better fix that."
How many times each day are statements like these uttered? These common expressions reveal our expectation that the government will take care of us. Because we demand it, our elected representatives pass more and more laws. Rules and regulations are handed down so quickly that we can't keep up with them.

Beware of asking the government to do too much, for from this comes servitude. The government often acts like a parent telling us what is good for us or bad for us and passing laws to that effect. As long as what we do does not imperil life, liberty, and property we should be free to make choices, through and by the free will given us by God. Our laws should be a help, not a hindrance, in achieving the goals we establish for ourselves.

In 1850, a French economist and statesman, Frederic Bastiat, wrote *The Law*. It was a time when socialism was sweeping France. The French, too, wanted the government to take care of everything and guarantee them the good life. Bastiat wrote, "We hold from God the gift which includes all others. This gift is life—physical, intellectual, and moral life."[1] But life cannot maintain itself alone. The Creator of life has entrusted us with the responsibility of preserving, developing, and perfecting it. In order that we may accomplish this, He has provided us with a collection of marvelous faculties.

And He has put us in the midst of a variety of natural resources. By the application of our faculties to these natural resources, we convert them into products and use them. This process is necessary in order that life may run its appointed course.

Life, faculties, production—in other words, individuality, liberty, property—this is man. And in spite of the cunning of artful political leaders, these three gifts from God precede all human legislation, and are superior to it. Life, liberty, and property do not exist because men have made laws. On the contrary, it was the fact that life, liberty, and property existed beforehand that caused men to make laws in the first place.[2]

Bastiat goes on to explain that a man has a natural right from God "to defend his person, his liberty, and his property." He further explains that our intelligence is but an outgrowth of our individuality, and property but an outgrowth of our intelligence. Ultimately, he defines the law as "the organization of the natural right of lawful defense. It is the substitution of a common force for individual forces. And this common force is to do only what the individual forces have a natural and lawful right to do; to protect persons, liberties, and properties; to maintain the right of each and to cause justice to reign over all." With this freedom we would succeed or fail on our own merit. We would take pride in our own achievements and accept responsibility for our own failures, not look to the vagaries of government for success or failure.

It must be noted that Bastiat saw, in 1848, only two issues that were a hindrance to the laws of the United States: slavery and tariffs. Slavery violated the law of liberty, and tariffs violated the laws of property. He said they were "a sorrowful inheritance from the Old World" and predicted that either could bring us ruin, as they perverted law. "The law has come to be an instrument of injustice," he wrote of America. As we know, slavery was one of the causes of the only war to be fought on our shores, and although slavery was abolished, the wounds from that war may never heal completely.

Asking a man or a government to take care of us in so many facets of our lives is leading our nation down a path to chaos. We make laws, alter laws, repeal laws as easily as the wind changes.

Our leaders claim good intentions, and I surely will not take issue with that. Rather, my complaint pertains to laws that don't work, and why these unprofitable laws continue to multiply.

Since the 1930s we have been gradually led to believe that the government will correct perceived wrongs and make all right in the world for us. It can't. It is a human institution. We must return wholeheartedly to our faith in Jesus Christ and the Father. John 1:1-5 should be the focus of strength in everything. "In the beginning was the word, and the Word was with God, and the Word was God. The same was in the beginning with God. All things were made by him; and without him was not any thing made that was made. In him was life; and the life was the light of men. And the light shineth in darkness; and the darkness comprehended it not."

Because of the promises of God, we can have security in our families, our nation, and our world. We are being constantly persuaded by the media that government is the wellspring from whence comes sustenance, clothing, shelter, and even hope! Through the world's religion of secular humanism, we are being hurled headlong away from our real hope and the giver of all good things, described in Matthew 6:25-34:

> Therefore I say unto you, Take no thought for your life, what ye shall eat, or what ye shall drink; nor yet for your body, what ye shall put on. Is not the life more than meat, and the body than raiment? Behold the fowls of the air: for they sow not, neither do they reap, nor gather into barns; yet your heavenly Father feedeth them. Are ye not much better than they? Which of you by taking thought can add one cubit unto his stature? And why take ye thought for raiment? Consider the lilies of the field, how they grow; they toil not, either do they spin: And yet I say unto you, That even Solomon in all his glory was not arrayed like one of these. Wherefore, if God so clothe the grass of the field, which today is, and tomorrow is cast into the oven, shall he not much more clothe you, O ye of little faith? Therefore take no thought, saying, What shall we eat? or, What shall we drink? or, wherewithal shall we be clothed? For after all these things do the Gentiles seek: for your heavenly Father knoweth that ye have need of these things. But seek ye first the kingdom of God, and his righteousness; and all these things shall be added unto you. Take therefore no thought for the morrow; for the morrow shall take thought for the things of itself. Sufficient unto the day is the evil thereof.

The Testaments tell us that God is the provider of all good things. We accept this emotionally in the innermost depths of our souls. Not many of us have had to stand in lines hour after hour for a loaf of bread. The United States has been a cornucopia of plenty to her people and to many other nations as well. We live in a nation of abundance such as the world has ever known. This is not a cause for guilt, but rather cause for having a thankful heart and a generous heart.

In the founding colonies it took superhuman effort to survive. One of the colonies went so far as to hold everything in common. Just as communism has collapsed, so did this policy at Jamestown/Plymouth. The problem was that not everyone thought he had to work. Indolence grew and became so pronounced that it threatened the entire community's survival. The scripture is very specific about work and eating: "If a man will not work, neither should he eat" (II Thessalonians 3:10). Being slothful, indolent, and lazy won't fill the stomach. This verse says "will not;" the wording is very important. "Will not" indicates a choice and implies an avoidance of responsibility for one's self or one's family, which is also denounced in I Timothy, 5:8: "But if any provide not for his own, and specially for those of his own house, he hath denied the faith, and is worse than an infidel."

Unfortunately, there are times when one has no choice, due to causes such as illness, inability to find work, or lack of education. Sometimes people cannot work. Are they to go hungry, unsheltered, and unfed? No. James 2:16 tells us, "And one of you say unto them, Depart in peace, be ye warmed and filled; notwithstanding ye give them not those things which are needful to the body; what doth it profit?" And Galatians 6:10 adds, "As we have therefore opportunity, let us do good unto all men, especially unto them who are of the household of faith." Those who have, must help those who have not, when there is need and when circumstances are beyond the needy's control.

Matthew 6:1-4 also tells us the proper spirit in which to give help:

> Take heed that ye do not your alms before men, to be seen of them: otherwise ye have no reward of your Father which is in heaven. Therefore when thou doest thine alms, do not sound a trumpet before thee, as the hypocrites do in the synagogues and in the streets,

that they may have glory of men. Verily I say unto you, They have their reward. But when thou doest alms, let not thy left hand know what thy right hand doeth: that thine alms may be in secret: and thy Father which seeth in secret himself shall reward thee openly.

In our plenty, we should rejoice and thank God when we have opportunity to help. Throughout the Bible, we are admonished to give comfort and aid to the poor. Leviticus 19:9-10 instructs us, "And when ye reap the harvest of your land, thou shalt not wholly reap the corners of thy field, neither shalt thou gather the gleanings of thy harvest. And thou shalt not glean thy vineyard, neither shalt thou gather every grape of thy vineyard; thou shalt leave them for the poor and the stranger: I am the Lord your God." Note that the poor had to work to gather their food. We learn from this fact that we must remember not to give too much. We can overdo it. We can give so much that we destroy the recipient's pride, lowering their initiative so that they become takers and not receivers. What is the difference between taking and receiving? Attitude. Put simply, a receiver will thank and reciprocate when able or when opportunity presents itself. It doesn't necessarily take the same form as the original assistance or aid, but it will be of worth both to the giver and recipient. Conversely, a taker receives what is given, then asks for more and more until he no longer asks but finally demands; and if his demands are not met, he will literally, not just figuratively, take, insisting that it is his right to do so. Thus, Christians must sometimes walk a fine line, or we enable people to ignore their responsibilities to themselves, their families, and their community.

The scriptures illustrate the results of indolence. Proverbs 24:30-34: "I went by the field of the slothful, and by the vineyard of the man void of understanding; And, lo, it was grown over with thorns, and nettles had covered the race thereof, and the stone wall thereof was broken down. Then I saw, and considered it well: I looked upon it, and received instruction. Yet a little sleep, a little slumber, a little folding of the hands to sleep: So shall thy poverty come as one that traveleth; and thy want as an armed man."

As citizens of the United States, we should not be lulled into the belief that government can "fix" everything, for in doing so we run the risk of becoming takers. In truth, the government doesn't even have any money, nor can it create it. By our labor, money is created. It is only the representation of hours spent by people, laboring and working physically and mentally. The only money the government has is received through the taxation of its citizens.

In 1932 the world was in the throes of a deep economic depression. Franklin D. Roosevelt became the president of the United States, and across the Atlantic Ocean the Weimar Republic came to an end. With its end came the rise of Nazi Germany led by Adolph Hitler. He became their elected leader on March 31, 1932. How were an intelligent people, blessed with an enduring work ethic, seduced by a man who wrought such evil? He worked hard. He seduced by words and aggravated the national problems when he could. He studied and exerted himself and eventually turned himself into a martyr for national socialism. While in prison he wrote *Mein Kampf.*

Hitler also encouraged people to put their faith in the government. Circumstances were wretched in Germany. First came hyperinflation, and then the world depression followed. People literally could not *carry* enough money to buy the family groceries. The German people had been humiliated by the Treaty of Versailles, which ended World War I, and Hitler preyed on their nationalism and their pride. There were several contributing factors, including unrest due to the influence of communism and general lawlessness. But Hitler came to power due to one overriding issue: The people believed he could return them to the good old days of economic prosperity and the power that issues from it. They wanted the good life; instead they reaped a whirlwind.

The people voted their pocketbooks and ultimately lost everything. They pretended that the evils, the excesses, the concentration camps didn't exist. It wasn't only Jews who were imprisoned, tortured, and murdered, but also people of so-called "inferior" races, Gypsies, and Christians who dared to speak out.

First-century history also has a lesson to be examined. Caligula, Claudius, and Nero ruled during the life of Paul. They, like our Congress, were big spenders. They bribed and bought with their own special "entitlement" programs. They taxed heavily, and inflation was the order of the day. In the book *Bankruptcy 1995*, Harry E. Figgie, Jr., writes, "In one thirty-year period during the third century A.D., for example, the price of wheat rose 100,000 percent. A loaf of bread that cost the equivalent of $2.00 at the beginning of the period cost $2,000 at the end." The great Roman Empire has been said to have collapsed because it was evil. This is true, but the evil extended from and to its rulers and their excesses. Their motto should have been "If we want it, we get it." The same slogan certainly would apply to our leadership today. Where is the moral fiber of our founding fathers? Where is the assurance and confidence of doing right; the humility of an upright custodian? We must not look the other way; we must no longer fool ourselves. We must not fear and by doing so become paralyzed. "All that is necessary for the triumph of evil, is that a good man do nothing."[3]

As important as money is in this world, we must keep it in its place. If we are diligent at work, not filled with false pride about job suitability, honest in our dealings with our fellow man, if we respect authority and are not given to vanity, we will have everything we need. God has promised, and he will provide. The burden is on us to accept His promise. Accepting His promise frees us immeasurably to live happy, productive lives. We will not be bound to the tyranny of fear, fear that causes us to make poor decisions about work, giving, or national leaders.

I opened this chapter with comments about how the government should "do" something, "fix" something. Actually, it should. It should fix itself. Due to the profligate behavior of many of our elected officials, we have endured scandal after scandal. Often, their admittedly immoral behavior has shamed us as a nation of law-abiding citizens.

How can we expect men who cannot master their own behavior to govern us? Still, we return them to office year after year. In doing so, don't we become a party to their immorality? Do we truly believe that there is a difference between a small lie and a big lie; a small theft and a big theft? Do we really believe that the semantics of words can change stealing to "overdrafts"? We are not so simpleminded. We know. The question is: Do we choose to know, or would we rather choose to pretend we don't know? If the answer is the latter, then we are ourselves culpable for government misbehavior. The German people were not held guiltless for what their leaders did.

An election can turn on one vote. We have choice in our country still, and we have a responsibility before God. As private citizens we are concerned about our monthly bills and try earnestly to live within our means. One hundred dollars means a lot to most of us—the weekly food bill, a doctor's bill, the electric bill—but we have people in our legislatures and our Congress who have seen fit to spend what we cannot even imagine. The minimum wage as enacted by the Congress is currently $5.15 per hour. If the national debt is more than $5 trillion, then each man, woman, and child in this country owes an estimated $20,000. When the government sells its bonds, it euphemistically calls it re-funding. Nobody is getting anything back. The government is literally borrowing more for us to pay back. We are already in servitude for the future, and we are being led to our own slaughter. We must be vigilant and prayerful. Give everything to Him and remember Psalm 127:1: Except the Lord build the house, they labor in vain that build it; except the Lord keep the city, the watchman watcheth but in vain. And Proverbs 14:34-35: "Righteousness exalteth a nation: but sin is a reproach to any people. The king's favour is toward a wise servant: but his wrath is against him that causeth shame."

Government leaders are supposed to serve by our consent and at our pleasure. They are supposed to work for us, but it is becoming increasingly evident that we are working for them. Government needs to return to its original purpose, to preserve and protect, not its current policy of interference and rule through excessive legislation. We are being oppressed by a policy of "management and control." We need to say no to politicians through our ballots and return to some common sense.

CHAPTER TEN

Special Interests: An Excess of Power

Political Action Committees are often justifed as an outgrowth of democracy. They are instead a perversion of freedom. The election laws regulating gifts and donations by individuals, corporations, and institutions are a threat to the rights of the common man. Our representatives in government are in their places of authority by the consent and will of the governed acting in concert with their natural rights and the United States Constitution. The PACs have contravened the law of equality and consent by bringing external forces to bear upon those who hold office. The men and women are precisely that, men and women. They have authority through the consent of the people, but all too often, this authority becomes translated as power, not stewardship. There are too many examples of this to enumerate, but they are known, recognized, and perceived at every level of government.

Mankind, by its very nature, is easily persuaded by the power or love of money. No one, no president, no senator, no representative, no man is above the law of the nation. Bribery is not the order of the day in the generally accepted definition, but bribery does not lend itself to only one form. It does not have to be an envelope of money. No, bribery can also withhold something of value or imply a threat to withhold. In this time of extensive Madison Avenue merchandizing of candidates for office, Political Action Committees have become very important financially and as persuaders of their members. The average citizen is consequently disenfranchised, and the influence of a few organizations grows disproportionately enormous. The one man–one vote principle was grounded in the belief that each man, not wealth, not land, nor any other persuading factor would be the measure of a man's consent and approval. When any PAC gives support materially or implied, the one man—one vote principle has been trampled. No principle, no matter how highly esteemed, should be given preferential treatment based on the power of influence of Political Action Committees, nor should political favor go to any particular corporation, company, or any other public, private, or civic institution.

Let the issues be decided on the merits, the pros and cons. The undue pressures exerted upon men and women places them in unfair positions lowering the respect they should have, and treats them in a such a manner that their minds and hearts are more likely to be for sale to the highest bidder. Contributions to political campaigns should be restricted to individuals. The condition currently exists that they are so busy pleasing this group or that, both national and foreign, that the true "common good" of the people is not being served.

Would it not be a virtue to remove these external pressures and the "dangling carrot" of money so that they would be freed from the constant necessity and burden of paying obeisance to special interests and return to representation "of, by, and for the people" and the "common good"?

James Madison, writing about the nature of property in 1792, said, "Property.... In the former sense, a man's land or merchandise, or money, is called his property. In the latter sense, a man has a property in his opinions and the free communication of them.... He has an equal property in the free use of his faculties, and free choice of the objects on which to employ them. In a word, as a man is said to have a right to his property, he may be equally said to have a property in his rights. Where an excess of power prevails, property of no sort is duly respected. No man is safe in his opinions, his person, his faculties, or his possessions. Where there is an excess of liberty, the effect is the same.... Government is instituted to protect property of every sort.... This being the end of government."[1]

Thus it is realized that the reasoning mind of the individual is being denied in favor of the collective will of groups exercising "an excess of power" and "an excess of liberty."[2] The rule of the majority opinion and or opinions are being subverted by special interests so that governance by majority subsequently becomes governance by minority, the result being, that elitist groups are created de facto and the rights of the average man have been abrogated to those claiming superior intellect or superior powers of reasoning and understanding. The non-elected few are made rulers of us all. The authorities (by consent) thus no longer pay heed to their constituents generally, but to groups, specifically. The ensuant feeling of distrust of those in positions of power are at once logical and reasonable. The insinuated power of a few over the many is a betrayal of our constitution, our natural rights, and the principles of free men coming together in order to form a union of self-governance. If this pattern continues, not only our material goods bur our individuality, our very personhood, is in jeopardy. The restriction of this power over legislators and the denial of this unconstitutional exercise of control would render this "excess of power" void of influence. A state of equilibrium could return so that the principle of "one man, one vote" could again resume its rightful importance in the land.

John Locke said, "But though this be a state of liberty, yet it is not a state of license."[3] Let us withdraw this "license" and return to our former liberty for the good of all.

CHAPTER ELEVEN

Taxes: Socialism and Plunder

In *The Law,* Bastiat quoted Mr. de Montalembert: "We must make war on socialism," Montalembert said, meaning, "We must make war against plunder."[1] Bastiat explains that man "may live and satisfy his wants by seizing the property of the labors of others . . . for the benefit of the person who makes the law, and in proportion to the power that he holds." That is what is happening via the pressure put upon elected officials by special interests.

Special interests pit group against group and one economic class against another economic class. It is the classic prescription for collectivism, as advocated by Marx and socialism. Since many people believe that the government is supposed to maintain their welfare, legislators have worked to pacify them with the "least possible effort." As a consequence, people may want to stop the legal plunder, or worse, they may want to participate in its supposed benefits. Bastiat's most important point is that socialism "erases from every one's conscience the distinction between justice and injustice." Absolutes are destroyed, and eternal truths are no longer considered eternal nor true.

What is plunder? It is nothing more than taking property from people and giving it to others. One group benefits "at the expense of another by doing what the citizen himself cannot do without committing a crime." Entitlements become what Bastiat called "acquired rights"; they are "legal plunder." Once again, morality collides with legality; civil laws are in conflict with natural law and spiritual law.

It is interesting to note what Bastiat believed constituted legal plunder and to see if those things exist in the United states today.

Bastiat	United States
tariffs	yes
benefits	yes
protection	yes
subsidies	yes
progressive taxation	yes
public (government) schools	yes
guaranteed jobs	no
guaranteed profits	no
minimum wages	yes
a right to relief	yes
a right to the tools of labor	yes[2]

These are the elements of a welfare state, and guaranteed health care, higher education, and job training threaten to be added. No doubt child care provided by government money (your taxes) will also come soon.

As I have pointed out earlier, there are many things that appear to be good but are instead evil. Socialism is one of them. Whereas the law should "be just; it must [now] be philanthropic."[3] We are guaranteed "life, liberty, and the pursuit of happiness" in freedom. Now the government has chosen our morality and we are under compulsion to obey.

Current laws are in contradiction to the preamble of the constitution. And current economic policies of taxation for certain government programs contravene the law of love; everything is now based on abject materialism. We hear taxes called "contributions." Contributions are not something given grudgingly or under compulsion. Words are being twisted to give the appearance of the moral laws of nature and of Scripture, the appearance of justice. We have been lulled to sleep by propaganda; if you tell people a lie long enough, they are eventually no longer able to recognize the truth.

Some taxes are justified and are not a part of plunder. Taxes for roads, bridges, national defense, the salaries of government employees and representatives are useful for the common good and do promote the "general welfare"; but when progressive taxation becomes a means of plunder and is in reality regressive, we have the right and privilege to say so. As Christians, we must be in harmony with "law, honor, and justice."[3] Just law is the issue, for if socialist thinkers have altered law for their purpose, then to whose law do we appeal? By law we have the ballot, and it is through the ballot that we must make our appeal and work to elect men imbued with justice. As Christians, it is our role to "render to Caesar" and thereby bring no reproach upon the church.

Education has become an increasingly important factor in the job market. Before World War II, the minority went on to college, and now it is just the opposite; many go on to graduate studies after obtaining the bachelor's degree. College-education costs can exceed $80,000, without extras. Where education through high school was the norm, college education has now been accepted as the standard. Public funding of college tuition is increasingly called for and is becoming viewed as a right. Current suggestions include fulfilling a public-service commitment to "repay" government-subsidized college education.

This sounds very noble indeed, but there are some logical gaps and pitfalls to be noted. First, how many years of service would be required to repay the debt? Second, on what money will those in a new "civil service" live? Will they be "paid" a government stipend, thus negating repayment of the debt? What is the method of enforcement? Will there be enlistments or contracts? What would the penalty be for failure to honor such a contractual obligation?

This public-service plan reminds me of the early history of European immigration to America, when those who were poor indentured themselves as servants to others individuals in order to have passage to this country. It is the equivalent of self-imposed slavery to the government, sacrificing one's freedom of choice. Various factors would compete with this civil service, such as marriage, the birth of a child, or potential job offers. All these freedoms would be potentially denied in order that the young person serve the state. Other repercussions would likely become evident. Ultimately, anything that places an individual in debt to the state should be avoided. An impersonal government can become a tyrannical master.

The importance of retaining freedom in society was described eloquently by Samuel Adams: "In short, it is the greatest absurdity to suppose it in the power of one, or any number of men, at the entering into society, to renounce their essential natural rights, or the means of preserving those rights; when the grand end of civil government, from the very nature of its institution, is for the support, protection, and defense of those very rights; the principal of which, as is before observed, are life, liberty and property. If men, through fear, fraud, or mistake, should in terms renounce or give up any essential natural right, the eternal law of reason and the grand end of society would absolutely vacate such renunciation. The right to freedom being the gift of God almighty, it is not in the power of man to alienate this gift and voluntarily become a slave."[4]

Bastiat also tells us, "Thus the Law of Nature stands as an Eternal Rule to all Men, *Legislators* as well as others. The *Rules* that they make for other Men's Actions, must, as well as their own, and other Men's Actions, be conformable to the law of nature, i.e. to the Will of God, of which that is a Declaration, and the *fundamental law of nature being the preservation of Mankind,* no Human Sanction can be good, or valid against it"[5] [emphasis added].

We see many necessities of life taxed. States already have sales taxes that, when combined with "hidden" taxes, are exorbitant and can be readily called "plunder." Taxation of fuels is one of those hidden taxes. Is it right, is it moral, to tax the energy necessary for the functioning of modern society? As cited in the "Ten Pillars of Economic Wisdom," natural resources combined with our use of tools are necessary to sustain our lives and improve our quality of life. God gave natural resources to man and the ability to use them. Taxes placed on energy sources cause price increases on literally everything, no matter what veiled terms are used or how just it is made to seem. This arena of tax increase hurts the poor more than any other group, despite "tax credits." The essentials of life: food, water, clothing, and shelter, and transportation to work, increase in cost, because not only vehicular fuels grow more expensive, but so do fuels used to generate electricity for homes, shops, factories, and entertainment. Every addition of tax is passed on to consumers. No one escapes such an unjust tax. Since the cost of production is raised, there is no choice but to add it to retail costs. Companies are already under pressure to trim production costs, which has added people to the unemployment rolls. Worker productivity will have to increase even more if these taxes are added. The people are being duped.

Energy taxes will never decrease the federal budget deficit. They will add to it, because fewer people will have jobs and therefore will not be paying taxes. The effect will be lower receipts from income taxes and more people receiving jobless benefits. The budget deficit will actually increase. This result is obtained when any arbitrary taxation occurs. The economy cannot be "boosted" by taxation, only trodden under. Any tax that impedes or obstructs business, big or small, destroys opportunity. No tax increase has ever reduced the deficit. The only thing that reduces a deficit, as all people with common sense know, is to reduce or cut spending; something that most elected officials don't seem to comprehend, as made obvious by the House Banking scandal. Everyone wants to spend money belonging to someone else. The penal code is supposed to protect us from thieves, but there is a huge problem when legalized theft is the object of complaint. We need to wake up from the government-induced anesthesia, speak our minds, and use legal means (the ballot, telephone, letters) to stop it. We *can*.

In 1860 J. Wingate Thornton perfectly captured the spirit of freedom so fundamental to this nation:

> The baneful effects of exorbitant wealth, the lust of power, and other evil passions, are so inimical to a free, righteous government, and find such an easy access to the human mind, that it is difficult, if possible, to keep up the spirit of good government, unless the spirit of liberty prevails in the state.
>
> This spirit, like other generous growths of nature, flourishes best in its native soil. It has been engrafted, at one time and another, in various countries: in America it shoots up and grows as in its natural soil. Recollecting our pious ancestors, the first settlers of the country,—nor shall we look for ancestry beyond that period,—and we may say, in the literal sense, we are children, not of the bond woman,

but of the free. It may hence be expected that the exertions and effects of American liberty should be more vigorous and complete ... the slavery of a people is generally founded in ignorance of some kind or another; and there are not wanting such facts as abundantly prove the human mind may be so sunk and debased, through ignorance and its natural effects, as even to adore its enslaver, and kiss its chains. Hence knowledge and learning may well be considered as most essentially requisite to a free, righteous government.[6]

Chapter Twelve

Economics and the Battle for Freedom

There are two approaches to economics at war in the world today. One is free enterprise, and the other is collectivism. The free-enterprise system is called capitalism, and collectivism is called communism or socialism. Free enterprise is in accord with natural law and, simultaneously, spiritual law. The other denies man's nature and spiritual law and wreaks havoc upon the people and their governments. The characteristics of these two systems are compared below. In studying them, you will find they are antithetical to each other. One espouses freedom, whereas the other uses uplifting arguments to justify the creation of near slavery. It is again a case of good versus evil. Certainly, socialism often arises from good intentions. But intentions are less important than results. If good intentions themselves had economic value, we would all be rich indeed. Unfortunately, as capitalism is weakened in the U.S. by socialistic policies, we are becoming poorer day by day, unable to satisfy the demands of the federal government.

Let us examine these two competing systems in more detail:

Socialism, Communism— Collectivism, Marxism	Christianity — Free Enterprise
1. Man is matter in motion	1. Man is in the image of God
2. Personality destroyed for sake of state	2. Respect for human personality

3. Respect for state; self-gratification	3. Self-respect
4. Reliance upon state planners	4. Self-reliance
5. Control by fear and force	5. Self-control, self-discipline
6. Men who oppose the leader are sacrificed	6. Justice for all—by law
7. Men regimented	7. Men free to dream, plan and venture
8. Talents represented to fit the pattern	8. Talents developed and used
9. No incentive for thrift and industry	9. Thrift and industry encouraged
10. No reward—payment for bare needs	10. Reward according to application
11. Obedience forced	11. Individual responsibility assumed
12. No basis for virtue	12. Virtue taught and practiced.[1]

The future depends upon today's battle, as outlined in the following choices:

1. Type of government—free or dictatorial
2. Type of economic system—free market or managed
3. Man in society—free or slave.[2]

It is important to note that although many communist governments have fallen, the values they embodied have taken root throughout Western society. If we examine collectivist thought closely, we can see this relationship:

COLLECTIVISM:	TODAY BECOMES:
1. Man is matter in motion	1. Secular humanism, New Age movement, New World Order, etc.
2. Personality destroyed for sake of state	2. Politically correct speech
3. Respect for state; self-gratification	3. Manmade law that contradicts spiritual law
4. Reliance upon state planners	4. Planned and managed economy, Federal Reserve

5. Control by fear and force	5. Health care, Social Security, Medicare Medicaid, environmental policies
6. Men who oppose the leader are sacrificed	6. Special interests
7. Men regimented	7. Government regulation of business economy
8. Talents represented to fit the pattern	8. Government job-training programs
9. No incentive for thrift and industry	9. Progressive tax on income, energy, inheritance, purchases, confiscatory laws
10. No reward—payment for bare needs	10. Barely enough left from paychecks for necessities of life
11. Obedience forced	11. Environmental laws, OSHA, etc.
12. No basis for virtue	12. Immorality condoned by government.[3]

Marxist (socialist) philosophy has deliberately created and fostered class warfare, hatred, envy, and strife. Although today it is not referred to directly as Marxism, socialism is its child and has been nurtured through the gradual indoctrination of people not only in the United States but in a preponderance of the nations of the world. People have turned over their rights of self-determination to strong central governments. In the U.S. we can say, with justification, that we are no longer a republic philosophically. We now live in a managed economy—and it is being terribly mismanaged by groups and individuals who think they know better than we do. When they euphemistically call taxes "contributions" and plunder "sacrifice," they are deluding no one but themselves. Call exorbitant taxes what you will, they are still the theft of hard-earned money by the arrogant, greedy, humanistic few who have been in power in this nation. The taxes of the 1700s, which led to so much outrage in this land, were actually lower than they are today. A chart of governments and their political and economic paths illustrates the peculiar divergence this nation took more than 200 years ago:

Political and Economic Paths

Man has spent most of his time on earth under GOVERNMENT CONTROL

COMMUNIST MANIFESTO written by Karl Marx and Frederick Engels in 1848—the cell from which came both Communism and Socialism

COMMUNIST REVOLUTION under Lenin in 1917—Bolsheviks, 40,000

1922, Mussolini in Italy, Fascist

1933, Hitler in Germany, Nazi (National Socialist) Party

In 1960 there are 1 million under Communist domination

Socialist trend in the United States

LIBERAL OR LEFT WING

CONSERVATIVE OR RIGHT WING

In 1776 DECLARATION OF INDEPENDENCE and CONSTITUTIONAL GOVERNMENT:
1. Government to be servant of the people, not the master.
2. People to control government, rather than government control people.
3. Freedom of religion.
4. Freedom of speech and of the press.
5. Freedom to own property.
6. Freedom to work and compete.
7. Freedom to choose type of work and to develop talents.
8. Freedom to dream and plan for individual advancement without government intervention.

—Dr. F. W. Mattox; reprinted by permission

Socialism (communism) was tested in our nation when it consisted of isolated communities, widely spread across the land. The Plymouth colony was founded under a patent (contract) whose ten articles instituted a socialistic arrangement. For the first seven years, all profits from "trade, traffic, trucking, working, fishing, or any means of any person or persons, remained still in the common stock." After the seven years, all "capital and profits, viz., the houses, lands, goods and chattels," were to be divided between the colonists and merchant adventurers. The colonists had hoped to work two days each week for themselves, but this article was stricken from the agreement, along with another, which would have given them their homes, "gardens, and home lots." Under the patent, they were being treated as "thieves and bond slaves," not "honest men." They were to have all necessities out of the "common stock and goods of the said colony." Over one-half died, leaving fifty colonists after 1620–21. After the harvest of 1622, they realized matters could not continue in this way. Land for each household was set aside so that famine would not decimate their numbers the following year. The colonists became much more industrious, for now their survival depended on themselves and was not left to someone else. The original contract, in denying the right to individual property, had simultaneously destroyed man's nature to work. Though Bradford and the early leaders didn't want to break the agreement, they realized that it was an article that disagreed with natural law and spiritual law. They wanted to live, responsible for themselves individually; this was their best and only hope.[4]

In 1647 Bradford wrote in his *History of Plymouth Plantation*, "the face of things was changed to the rejoicing of the hearts of many." Not only was hunger abated, but some even had corn to sell, and "any general want or famine" was not "among them."[5]

Jamestown was also to provide out of a common store. They suffered and endured famine, primarily because the majority of the people would not work. Out of 500 colonists in 1607, only 60 remained in 1610. In 1611 Sir Thomas Dale took a new course by allotting three acres to every man. Theft and lawlessness ceased to be a problem, and the Jamestown colony began to prosper. The socialist/communist policy of their original charter had not worked. With the return to free enterprise, Jamestown began its journey to freedom, economically.

Collectivism did not work for the young colonies and doesn't work now. Just as it encouraged indolence then, so it does now. Compare the planks of the Communist Manifesto of 1848 with the socialist planks below:

COMMUNIST PLANKS *Communist Manifesto* written by Karl Marx and Frederick Engels in 1848	SOCIALIST PLANKS of the Socialist Party
1. Government ownership (1) Factories (2) National Bank (3) Abolition of private lan ownership (4) Centralization of communication and transportation	1. Government ownership (1) Industry (2) Railroads (3) Banks (4) Land
2. Central planning of production	2. Government planning of production
3. Heavy progressive income tax	3. Heavy progressive income tax
4. Abolition of inheritance	4. Extremely heavy inheritance tax
	5. Government control of prices and wages
	6. Full employment and government control of medical services.[6]

Take special note of numbers 3, 4, 5, and 6. It would appear that the socialists are almost two-thirds of the way to their goal.

The words "socialism" and "communism" are used interchangeably by communists; the goals are the same. The only difference is in the method of reaching those goals. Communists favor reaching them by force and bullets; socialists generally favor reaching them by indoctrination and ballots. Prime Minister Harold MacMillan of Britain said: "Socialism gets you down bit by bit by a kind of anesthetic process. It might be called mercy killing. Communism just knocks you in the head."[7]

Yes, we have fallen asleep slowly. The anesthetic began to be adminstered in the 1930s, when President Hoover signed the Hawley

Smoot Tariff Bill, raising tariffs from 26 percent to 50 percent: other nations quickly retaliated through their own trade policies. Consequently, as the prices of foreign goods rose, Europe was laboring under the war reparations of World War I and couldn't sell as many products here—they were being pushed to the brink of financial collapse. In 1931 Hoover acquiesced to a one-year moratorium on reparations and debt payments. The Europeans went off the gold standard, selling their gold on our markets, which only increased our difficulties. In 1933 President Roosevelt began his 100 days of legislation, some of it passed in as few as four hours after being submitted. Where Hoover had begun the attack on the depression with aggressive taxation on imports, President Roosevelt began controlling production of the major crops: wheat, corn, cotton and four others. This was called the Agricultural Adjustment Act (May 1933). By controlling production, they sought to control prices. Farmers were paid (in citizens' tax dollars) not to plant. Crops such as wheat were plowed under in order to raise the price of wheat. The cost of bread could have been cheaper had this action not been taken—and people had precious little money. Although this sort of intervention is both unnatural and short-sighted, farm subsidies still continue today.

Also in the 1930s, the National Recovery Administration, enacting the National Industrial Recovery Act, created industrial regulations, established collective bargaining through unions, protected workers with wages and hours rules, and ended child labor. Despite the one good thing, ending child labor, the NRA failed. Strikes were mounted against non-union operations, and because the regulations were such a tangle, they caused price increases that made goods unaffordable to consumers. In 1935 the Supreme Court ruled against the NRA's codes. What followed was a litany of collectivist-inspired legislation: the CWA, TVA, NYA, NLRB, the Wayne Act, and the Social Security Act. In 1937 the president tried to "pack" the Supreme Court and suffered a biting defeat of 70–22 in the Senate. By 1942 it became a moot question, as only two of the original justices remained on the court.

The New Deal was the beginning of the socialist trend in the United States, and all this collectivist legislation didn't end the national economic troubles, nor did it help the people generally. In 1937 the economic difficulties renewed, which led to the Fair Labor Standards Act (1938), instituting the minimum wage. Violence increased as labor unions grew in strength. Union membership tripled from 1932 to 1941.

While some called the New Deal progressive, others called it socialism. One thing is certain, however: It gave the federal government the responsibility of solving problems by creating a managed economy. Government spending was viewed as the material salvation of the American people.

Taking a closer look at the minimum wage law, the sacred cow of the labor movement, illustrates why government-managed economics don't make sense in practice, no matter how good their intentions may be. In 1938 the minimum was set at 25 cents, when the average wage was already 63 cents per hour. Historically, the minimum wage has always been below the average hourly wage, so that the minimum wage plays catch-up with existing wages. These arbitrary minimums actually work against employment by artificially determining the value of the worker. Wages are determined by the productiveness of an employee, not by government fiat. In a 1993 *New York Times* article by Peter Passel, we learn that "myriad studies have confirmed that employers respond to wage regulation by cutting their payrolls; most put the damages at roughly a one percent loss in jobs for a 10 percent increase in the minimum."[8] Most households could not subsist on minimum wages. At the current $5.15 per hour, a full-time, forty-hour-per-week employee would earn $206 a week. After Social Security and income tax deductions, what is left would barely buy groceries.

Mostly teenagers fall into the minimum wage group, and teens are already being supported by their parents. The minimum wage is no incentive for those on welfare to enter the workforce, since they can get more from assistance programs than they can by working.[9] This is an indictment of both minimum wage laws and a welfare system.

The higher the minimum wage rises, the smaller the workforce becomes, and employees are, of necessity, forced to become more productive to justify their wages and benefits. A company is not going to employ two people when the work can be accomplished by one. It is better to hire one productive employee for $7 per hour plus benefits rather than two employees for a total of $10.30 (two hours of work at minimum wage) plus benefits for two. Productivity is the key to wages and the reason for employment. From the New Deal sprang the central government interventionist policies we labor under today. Some of the legislation has been good, some bad—that is not the real issue. The real issue is that the people have been manipulated to reject the acceptance of personal responsibility. A paternalistic government is in place, with the apparent approval of the citizens. We need to return to the solid foundations of economic security and not depend on the vagaries of an impersonal government that cannot see individuals. There comes a time when children grow up and don't need parental care. We should act like adults and reject the largesse of an imitation parent that cannot measure up. We should not expect government to take care of us.

The American Economic Foundation was incorporated in 1939. This organization publishes a wonderful book called *How We Live: A Simple Dissection of the Economic Body*, based on the "Ten Pillars of Economic Wisdom" by Fred G. Clark and Richard S. Rimanoczy. These "Ten Pillars" are easily understood and above all easily practiced if one will only take time to learn and use them. They are the basics of free enterprise and individual freedom. Here is a formula that outlines the basis for the pillars: "Man's material welfare (MMW) equals his natural resources (NR) plus his muscular and mental human energy (HE) multiplied by the efficiency of his tools (T). Thus, MMW = NR + HE x T." And here are the pillars themselves:

TEN PILLARS OF ECONOMIC WISDOM

1. Nothing in our material world can come from nowhere or go nowhere, nor can it be free: everything in our economic life has a source, a destination, and a cost that must be paid.

2. Government is never a source of goods. Everything produced is produced by the people, and everything that government gives to the people, it must first take from the people.

The piper will be paid. Pillars one and two explain that nothing suddenly appears out of thin air. We talk of a "free lunch," but that is an illusion. When one seeks medical care, one finds a doctor who spent eight years in school at a cost of approximately $200,000; one finds modern technology developed by researchers and scientists from every sphere of expertise from engineering to computers, all educated at a cost. Drugs had to be researched and developed by educated people, production costs had to be met, and salaries were paid to the workers who make, package, and deliver these products. Then there is the pharmacist who dispenses the medicine. Every step involves an exchange of labor for money. Everything material has a cost, and government cannot change that. If the government provides all of this, they have to pay the same costs you do, and to pay these costs they will have to take your money first in order to provide it to others. The government "gives" nothing. Someone, somewhere, is paying.

3. The only valuable money that government has to spend is that money taxed or borrowed out of the people's earnings. When government decides to spend more than it has thus received, that extra unearned money is created out of thin air, through the banks, and when spent, takes on value only by reducing the value of all money, savings, and insurance.

We all know that the government has been living beyond its means, which technically means, beyond our means. The government has an advantage: a printing press. When the government gets $100 in taxes but spends $120, the extra $20 is created out of thin air by reducing the value of $100 to approximately $83.33. The result is that you might still have $100 bill, but its value has been reduced to 83 percent. The ultimate value of money is not the numerical value on its face, but what it will buy. Money is only a medium of exchange, a representation of one's labor and work, mental or physical. If prices go up, people don't buy, and layoffs and recession occur.

4. In our modern exchange economy, all payroll and employment come from customers, and the only worthwhile job security is customer security. If there are no customers, there can be no payroll and no jobs.

5. Customer security can be achieved by the worker only when he cooperates with management in doing the things that win and hold customers. Job security, therefore, is a partnership problem that can be solved only in a spirit of understanding and cooperation.

"The customer is always right" is a good interpretation of pillar four. When the price of a product exceeds its perceived value, the customer will not or cannot make the purchase. The product must have the quality that meets the customer's standards yet be priced competitively, or the customer will go elsewhere. When customers increasingly go to competitors, job security is threatened. When people make a purchase, part of the cost is in the manufacture of the goods, but another portion of the cost pays the employee, his social security, unemployment taxes, other benefits, plus company or corporate taxes. It behooves employees to help management turn out the best possible products and to give courteous service to every potential customer. By doing so, they increase their personal job security. The lazy employee doesn't hurt just the company which employs him, but every fellow employee as well.

6. Because wages are the principal cost of everything, widespread wage increases, without corresponding increases in production, simply increase the cost of everybody's living.

7. The greatest good for the greatest number means, in its material sense, the greatest goods for the greatest number, which in turn means the greatest productivity per worker.

When we purchase refrigerators, for instance, we don't ponder where the metals, plastics, or glass originated. Miners, steel fabricators, the cost of the manufacturing equipment, the transport of all the materials in every phase of production, the energy used, the sellers (company and employees), taxes along the way, insurance costs—all of these contribute to the final price of a refrigerator or any other product. If any one employee gets an increase in wages, all the attendant parts of his salary go up (Social Security taxes and unemployment taxes). The result is that the retail price increases unless the employee increases his production. Example: A widget costs $1,000 to manufacture per unit. The employees get a raise. To retain the price, he must make one additional unit for every ten units.

$1,000 (cost per unit)	$1,000 (cost per unit)
x	x
10 (number of units)	11 (number of units)
$10,000 (cost for 10 units)	$11,000 (cost for 11 units)

The cost per unit remains constant with increased production. If the price does not remain constant, the cost of living rises for each person. Finally, when the widget-maker goes to buy a widget, his raise will be taken by the rise in cost to $1100. Thus, he has not profited from a raise in wages. If a worker can produce eleven widgets a week instead of ten per week, eleven people will buy a widget at $1,000, as opposed to perhaps only eight people at $1100, because two of the original ten may have been priced out of the market, making a net loss for the company. For wages to increase, productivity must increase.

8. All productivity is based on three factors: (1) natural resources, whose form, place, and condition are changed by the expenditure of (2) human energy (both muscular and mental), with the aid of (3) tools.

9. Tools are the only one of these three factors that man can increase without limit, and tools come into being in a free society only when there is a reward for the temporary self-denial that people must practice in order to channel part of their earnings away from purchases that produce immediate comfort and pleasure, and into new tools of production. Proper payment for the use of tools is essential to their creation.

Natural resources do not come ready to use. Most are taken out of the ground in an unusable form. Tools, trucks for transport, furnaces for smelting, refineries for oil, factories for manufacturing, all are part of the chain of human labor that transforms a raw material into a usable product for the consumer. Everything we buy and sell requires the use of tools for production, coupled with man's mental and physical energy. Tools aren't just things such as hammers, nails, plows and tractors. When you wake up in the morning you begin using tools immediately. The lamps, the coffee pot, the stove, and the radio are all tools, and the use of tools continues all day. Telephone systems, computers, vehicles (cars, trucks, trains, airplanes, and boats), and even the lowly pencil are all tools. We cannot live well without tools. They increase our productivity and raise our standard of living. The most basic example of increased productivity through the use of tools is farming. Before the invention of modern equipment such as tractors, balers, combines, and a myriad of other farm equipment, it was hard continuous work to plow, seed, and harvest just forty acres. With the invention and manufacture of efficient equipment, a man can work many times that amount of acreage. But tools are not created out of nothing. They, too, require natural resources and man's workmanship in order to exist. Some cost little, and some cost dearly. Their value to man in increasing his productivity is incontrovertible. They increase both the speed of our work and its quality. All the inventions and workmanship of man are the cause of our quality of life being on such a high plane. The farmer who saves or borrows to buy more equipment that increases his productivity has invested wisely, for his tools will repay him by increasing his production without increasing time expended. This is true in farming, manufacturing, and in every facet of life that involves expenditure of energy.

10. The productivity of the tools—that is, the efficiency of the human energy applied in connection with their use—has always been highest in a competitive society in which the economic decisions are made by millions of progress-seeking individuals, rather than in a state-planned society in which those decisions are made by a handful of all-powerful people, regardless of how well-meaning, unselfish, sincere, and intelligent those people may be.

Where the minds of people are free to invent and design, progress moves forwards, raising the quality of life. We have all witnessed what the command economy of the U.S.S.R. did to Eastern Europe and parts of Asia. People were not free to explore and create. This is not just a phenomenon of communism but is found in all collectivist/socialist societies. Only when man is free of the shackles of government-directed economies is he totally free to pursue the decisions for his personal well-being and thereby increase his contributions to society generally. The good intentions of centralized government can never replace the mind of the individual in the determination of what is of worth and value in man's pursuit of happiness.

CHAPTER THIRTEEN

Equality, Perception, and Faith

In England during the middle 1600s, a group of Puritans known as "the Levellers" sought the recognition of the equality of mankind. They presented a document, "The Agreement of the People," which was to be a new constitution for the English people. It would have given the ballot to men, thereby instituting consent of the governed. There was one very small radical subgroup called "the Diggers" among the Levellers, who sought to go further.

The Levellers believed in the equality of man under God's grace in religious matters. Using the scriptures as their model, political democracy was their goal. The Diggers, by contrast, sought a radical end of unstructured government and a communal economy. The Diggers were proto-communists, the forerunners of Karl Marx.

The inherent problem with the Diggers and with communism was the denial of man's natural right to his property and his freedom to dispose of property, according to his free will, bound only by the "the law of Nature"[1] and in accordance with the revealed law of God.

It was at this period of history that John Locke lived and worked. Locke understood the principles of democracy from the Word and natural law. In Chapter II of his *Treatise Concerning Civil Government*, the nature of man and his equality is his overriding theme. Locke states "That all men by nature are equal," and he also offers early arguments for the equality of women. In chapter seven he quotes Exodus 20:12, "Honour thy father and thy mother: that thy days may be long upon the land which the Lord thy God giveth thee"; and Ephesians 6:1, "Children, obey your parents in the Lord: for this is right." In Locke's view, these and other scriptures showed the equality of husband and wife, mother and father, for they both were to be obeyed equally.

Man's equality does not reside in material possessions, but within the person, that unique individual and special person who is like no other. We are each marked and identifiable by our genetic structure. We are truly unique, and as David said in Psalm 139:14-16, "I will praise thee; for I am fearfully and wonderfully made: marvelous are thy works; and that my soul knoweth right well. My substance was not hid from thee, when I was made in secret, and curiously wrought in the lowest parts of the earth. Thine eyes did see my substance, yet being unperfect; and in thy book all my members were written, which in continuance were fashioned, when as yet there was none of them." The scriptures tell us, too, that we are equal no matter our race or creed: "There is neither Jew nor Greek, neither male nor female: for ye are all one in Christ Jesus"(Galatians 3:28); and "Where there is neither Greek nor Jew, circumcision nor uncircumcision, Barbarian, Scythian, bond nor free: but Christ is all, and in all" (Colossians 3:11).

Equality is not external; it is an internal acceptance of one's worth and value. It is the condition of man's soul and mind that permit him to move, to live, to work in the absence of fear. Many groups and individuals incorrectly perceive that they must labor and/or fight for equality. This is a tragic waste of human energy. God has given equality to man through his gift of free will. Just as we can accept or reject Christ, we can accept or reject our equality.

If we assume that our perceptions are always valid, we run the risk of lying to ourselves, thereby denying our powers of reason, and consequently we hide the truth from ourselves. Earlier I quoted Cicero: "True law is right reason in agreement with nature." Someone suffering from anorexia nervosa is a prime example of failure to employ "right reason" and therefore failing to see the truth. Anorexics can look in the mirror and view the evidence of their physical state, but through a delusion present in the mind, they either do not see what is there or do not believe what they see.

They hold to the false belief that they are "fat," unacceptable to themselves. The actual thing about them that could be thought unacceptable, however, is their false perception of the truth of their condition. The person isn't unacceptable. The falsehood is unacceptable. It is not reasonable. It does not agree with the observable. By extension, anyone who believes that they do not have equality in the world is failing to perceive the truth, that they are by nature equal to every other human being. These false beliefs block us from seeing ourselves as we are and recognizing our true worth. They also stand as barriers between us and other people, and between us and God. In fact, these false beliefs can prevent us from following God's Word: "Thou shalt love the Lord thy God with all thy heart, and with all thy soul, and with all thy mind. This is the first and great commandment. And the second is like unto it, Thou shalt love thy neighbor as thyself. On these two commandments hang all the law and the prophets" (Matthew 22:37-40).

A similar exhortation is found in Mark 12:29-31: "And Jesus answered him. The first of all the commandments is, Hear, O Israel; The Lord our God is one Lord: And thou shalt love the Lord thy God with all thy heart, and with all thy soul, and with all thy mind, and with all thy strength: this is the first commandment. And the second is like, namely this, Thou shalt love thy neighbor as thyself. There is none other commandment greater than these." If we obey part one of these commands, we are going to accept parts two and three. Loving God is more than saying, "I love God." It is an expression of faith and thanksgiving. It is an act of our free will involving our intellect working with the strength of our bodies striving to put Him first in our lives. It is also the acceptance of His promises in the Revealed Law. Love is trusting and believing. It is this belief in God's promises to us that gives us the freedom to love ourselves. He has told us our value, our worth, and His great love for us. When we accept and not do question it, we do not have to look to externals to show us our worth or prove our esteem. Loving Him and accepting His love teaches us love and acceptance of ourselves. Understanding our value to the Father teaches us that our fellow man is also of value and worth. To love our fellow man, we must love ourselves; and in turn, to love ourselves, we must love God. And to love God, we must believe Him. Love is not known by words only, but by the actions prompted by love. That some treat others as less than equal does not nullify equality. Equality is not a gift or whim of mankind. It resides with God, the giver of all good things.

Throughout the world today there are many who would deny equality to their fellow man. Slavery was, and in some societies still is, in practice. The flip side of this coin is the granting of special or extraordinary rights. These are imposed under the guise of laws that recognize the equality of all people. They are for special situations to rectify wrongs, or redress of grievances. Are they "right" law? No. The constitution accepts that all men are created equal, with the right to life, liberty, and the pursuit of happiness. These further laws can only serve to create a special class of citizens, the result being that they are either superior or inferior to the rest of the citizens. This is antithetical to the Constitution of the United States, the intent of the founding fathers, the common good, and the spirit of American jurisprudence.

The federal government is not the "great father" with the right to dispense equality or pronounce it to mankind. God has done both. Each man or woman must accept this individually. It is not a collective matter, for each group of people begins with individuals.

Equality must be viewed from two sides, however. As Locke states:

> But though this be a state of liberty, yet it is not a state of license; though man in that state have an uncontrollable liberty to dispose of his person or possessions, yet he has not liberty to destroy himself, or so much as any creature in his possession, but where some nobler use than its bare preservation calls for it. The state of Nature has a law of Nature to govern it, which obliges every one, and reason, which is that law, teaches all mankind who will but consult it, that being all equal and independent, no one ought to harm another in his life, health, liberty or possessions; for men being all the workmanship of one omnipotent and infinitely wise Maker; all the servants of one sovereign Master, sent into the world by His order and about His business; they are His property, whose workmanship they are made to last during His, not one another's pleasure.

Locke continues:

> And that all men may be restrained from invading others' rights,

and from doing hurt to one another, and the law of Nature be observed, which willeth the peace and preservation of all mankind, the execution of the law of Nature is in that state put into every man's hands, whereby every one has a right to punish the transgressors of that law to such a degree as may hinder its violation. For the law of Nature would, as all other laws that concern men in this world, be in vain if there were nobody that in the state of Nature had a power to execute that law, and thereby preserve the innocent and restrain offenders; and if any one in the state of Nature may punish another for any evil he has done, every one may do so. For in that state of perfect equality, where naturally there is no superiority or jurisdiction of one over another, what any may do in prosecution of that law, every one must needs have a right to do.

We are faced with the acceptance of our own equality and the equality of others. The most important characteristic of equality is conscience. It is man's freedom of choice in matters of conscience that gives us our greatest problem.

Man by free will can accept or reject God, Christ, and the Word. We cannot deny this freedom, because it is of God and to do so would contravene the laws of God. The founders of United States predicated this nation's existence upon His Word. This confirms that none are under the compulsion of man in matters of conscience. As we cannot compel, neither should the government compel God-believing people to act in contradiction to their consciences. This would be a violation of our equality under natural law, revealed law, and laws made by man, as represented in our Bill of Rights.

The threat of government compulsion is becoming a reality. Hawaii and New Jersey have enacted laws "prohibiting discrimination in the work-place based on sexual orientation." Massachusetts, Wisconsin, Connecticut, and the District of Columbia have similar laws. Georgetown University did legal battle in 1980 after the passage of the 1977 Human Rights Act. They refused to provide funding for homosexual societies. Georgetown University, existing under the auspices of the Catholic Church and accepting the injunctions of the Scriptures, was bound to its beliefs in this matter of conscience. They were sued. A reasoning person would assume, quite naturally, that the First Amendment in the "free exercise" clause would have sufficed. Not so. The appeals court ruled in 1987 that the university had to provide the same benefits to all organizations. They did not, however, have to be recognized "officially." Congress, in 1990, passed an amendment exempting "religious educational institutions."[2]

The equality of Christians in our democracy is in peril. If we hold to absolutes predicated on the Word of God, we are called bigots, hypocrites, fools, looked at askance, and seen as conspirators against the freedom of people; we are castigated for narrowness and perceived by many to be dictators. None of these could be further from the truth.

As Christians, the Word is inviolate and Christ is the Rock. All law is under Him. We are subject to the laws of government. That our freedom to believe and practice that which we understand to be God's will is our right as citizens of the United States. We must work diligently to preserve these rights. As others do not want their rights denied, we must be vigilant to see that our rights are secured.

CHAPTER FOURTEEN

Marriage:
A Pact With God

At this moment in history, we are balanced precariously, as if on the edge of a cliff. Using science and technology, we can stand on that edge and get a powerful view of the universe's miracles. On the other hand, adopting the skeptical, aspiritual scientific viewpoint, which admits no God, leads to moral erosion. We cannot rely solely on science to solve the problems we are facing today.

Smallpox, typhoid fever, and polio were once the scourges of mankind. And when the "Black Death," or Bubonic Plague, swept across Europe in the fourteenth century, it was so devastating that some villages were left completely uninhabited—up to half of Europe's population was lost. The plague was transmitted easily through casual contact, and it killed quickly. People lacked the scientific knowledge to halt the calamitous spread of the Bubonic Plague; thus, one could say that ignorance played a large part in the plague's deadly impact.

Today the world has a new plague: AIDS. Auto Immune Deficiency Syndrome is spreading at an exponential rate. This time, ignorance plays a smaller role. Instead, immorality drives the pandemic. AIDS is not selective. Faithful wives, innocent babies, hemophiliacs, health-care workers, all these and more are unwitting victims of this terminal virus. Although deviant sexual activity seems to have been the primary source of the epidemic, it is now passed through dirty needles, blood transfusions, and by blood from an infected person getting through a break or pore in the skin of another individual. The virus develops slowly and insidiously; consequently, many infected people infect others without knowing that they are even infected.

The so-called "sexual revolution" has given us more than we bargained for, and definitely not what was sought. People have ignored the principles of chastity, making the very laws of nature that would have prevented the current anguish turn back on us. Perhaps it should not surprise us that AIDS cuts across social lines, because our abandonment of morals reaches all structures of social order. In the past, our nation had laws outlining correct sexual behavior. It was not only immoral but illegal to participate in adultery, fornication, and sodomy. (Fortunately, there are still laws on the books against bestiality, pedophilia, and incest. One wonders how much longer they will stand.)

Our laws against these sexual practices did not originate in the minds of man. These ordinances originated with God. They were not burdensome laws, but laws that protected us in our ignorance. Yes, they were and are a protection to people everywhere, believer and non-believer. With all the diseases directly related to indiscriminate and promiscuous sexual activity, we should be grateful that the law of chastity was laid down for us. God was not cruel and selfish, but loving and generous, giving us rules of conduct and living that are for our protection physically and mentally.

God said in I Corinthians 6:9-11, "Know ye not that the unrighteous shall not inherit the kingdom of God? Be not deceived: neither fornicators, nor idolaters, nor adulterers, nor effeminate, nor abusers of themselves with mankind, Nor thieves, nor covetous, nor drunkards, nor revilers, nor extortioners, shall inherit the kingdom of God. And such were some of you: but ye are washed, but ye are sanctified, but ye are justified in the name of the Lord Jesus, and by the Spirit of our God."

In the NIV, any possibility of ambiguity due to alteration of word meanings in modern usage is eliminated: "Do you not know that the wicked will not inherit the kingdom of God? Do not be deceived: Neither the sexually immoral nor idolaters nor adulterers nor male prostitutes nor homosexual offenders nor thieves nor the greedy nor drunkards nor slanderers nor swindlers will inherit the kingdom of God. And that is what some of you were . . ."

In this day of "freedom," we have enslaved ourselves so gradually and insidiously that we are sliding into an abyss, devoid of common sense, happiness, health, joy, and life itself. We have destroyed the very thing we were chasing—freedom. Now we cannot open our newspapers, turn on television or radio, drive down the street, or open a magazine without being assaulted by sexual images. This overload is dulling our senses beyond recognition. In times past, we were startled and felt embarrassment or shame. Now we giggle or make silly remarks, or even worse, we feel nothing; we say nothing.

In our consumer-oriented society, sex has become one of the principal tools of advertising and sales promotion. Why? Why has sex become such an effective motivator? It didn't happen overnight. If sex is just an image, something for the senses, it becomes far too easy to use its power to distort our social values. We used to buy what we needed and wanted on the basis of value and usefulness. We wanted our money's worth. We didn't go deeply into debt; we didn't chase things to make us "feel good" about ourselves; we didn't devalue ourselves by feeling incomplete without "things." We have bought another "big lie"—that things give us value. We buy the latest fashions, with the primary consideration being how we will be perceived by other people, not because it is good for us, protects us, or represents a good value. We buy so much because it gets us attention and gives us a feeling of security in a world that measures our worth at a very shallow level.

We are in danger of trading our true worth for the externals of the world. We are made in the image of God Himself. There is our value, our worth, our being, and our hope. The advertising industry is not interested in us as individuals. It is a business, and its aim is to make money. That in itself is good. No one is in business to go broke or just break even. It is the result of their business methodology that is the cause for concern.

Did the commercial use of sexual imagery work on us gradually to sway our self imagery, or did a poor self-esteem make us receptive to such advertising? Yes, we do want to be stylish, neat, and clean, which are all desirable qualities. We want to be able to look in a mirror and be happy and approving of the reflection. We need, foremost, approval in order to feel secure. But it is important not to look outside ourselves for that approval. If we approve of ourselves in our innermost being, we don't need the approval of others, nor do we seek attention in inappropriate ways. By placing their authority outside themselves, people can be essentially programmed to believe they must have a certain look, buy a certain item, drink a particular beverage, or use a certain product in order to be accepted. The message is, "This item will bring fulfillment" and self-worth. If we go inside ourselves to find our answers, we will find God there, guiding us and giving us strength. That is fulfillment.

We have only two options. That which is good or that which is not. God's guidance, or false images. There is no middle ground. We either hold to that which is chaste and modest inwardly and outwardly, or we become inwardly corrupt and reflect this outwardly through our apparel and behavior. We must not cheapen, devalue, or degrade the honor with which we were created. We were created a "little lower than the angels" and in His image. He breathed into us the breath of life.

We must not defraud ourselves nor be deluded. We are in danger, as a nation, of worshipping the physical nature of man, perverting the use and function of the body, removing it from that which is holy. We are becoming idolaters of sex, prostitution, and lewdness, a people given over to carnal desires, which we pursue unrelentingly. No, not everyone is buying into this lie, but on a national level, the problem is pervasive and touches everyone. The life of our nation is at stake, and, most importantly, so are our souls.

How do we know a false image when we see it? We must remember what beauty really is. The dignity and grace of clean speech, kindness in manner, modesty, and respect for other people are among the most beautiful qualities any human possesses. We will lose these virtues if we permit the continued contamination of our daily lives.

Moral relativism leads us to set aside these virtues, which are born of absolutes—absolute faith and devotion to a Godly life. Scriptural law, as we have already seen, is not abstract but rooted in reality, in common sense. The repudiation of scriptural law leads to pain and anguish, because it is a flouting of natural law here on earth. Natural law will not be disobeyed without consequences. Natural Law is unchanging and immutable and is not subject to change any more than are the laws of God in scriptural matters. In fact, they operate hand in hand. The moral truths of God teach us about natural law; when obeyed, they protect us from the penalties exacted when we act in disharmony with nature. Consequently, the Word is the guide not only for our salvation in eternity but also teaches us how live under the laws of nature with safety. If we will only study and heed His injunctions, we will see many of our weaknesses, struggles, and pain eased in this life. He has provided our protection if we will but have the wisdom to heed His advice and laws. Just as earthly parents know how to give good gifts to their children, God has given us wisdom, knowledge, and spiritual advice that can create for us a more abundant life. We must acknowledge and use that gift.

The following scriptures tell us what God said about marriage:

- "Therefore shall a man leave his father and his mother, and shall cleave unto his wife: and they shall be one flesh" (Genesis 2:24).
- "None of you shall approach to any that is near of kin to him, to uncover their nakedness: I am the Lord. The nakedness of thy father, or the nakedness of thy mother, shalt thou not uncover: she is thy mother; thou shalt not uncover her nakedness. The nakedness of thy sister, the daughter of thy father, or daughter of thy mother, whether she be born at home, or born abroad, even their nakedness thou shalt not uncover" (Leviticus 18: 6-8).
- "Unto Adam also and to his wife did the Lord God make coats of skins, and clothed them" (Genesis 3:21).
- "Whoso findeth a wife findeth a good thing, and obtaineth favour of the Lord" (Proverbs 18:22).
- "Have ye not read, that he which made them at the beginning made them male and female, And said, For this cause shall a man leave father and mother, and shall cleave to his wife: and they twain shall be one flesh? Wherefore they are no more twain, but one flesh. What therefore God hath joined together, let man not put asunder" (Matthew 19:4-6).
- "Take ye wives, and beget sons and daughters; and take wives for your sons, and give your daughters to husbands, that they may bear sons and daughters; that ye may be increased there, and not diminished" (Jeremiah 29:6).
- "And I will betroth thee unto me forever; yea, I will betroth thee unto me in righteousness and in judgment, and in loving kindness, and in mercies" (Hosea 2:19).
- "Nevertheless, to avoid fornication, let every man have his own wife, and let every woman have her own husband. Let the hus-

band render unto the wife due benevolence: and likewise also the wife unto the husband. The wife hath not power of her own body, but the husband: and likewise also the husband hath not power of his own body, but the wife. Defraud ye not one the other, except it be with consent for a time, that ye may give yourselves to fasting and prayer; and come together again, that Satan tempt you not for your incontinency" (I Corinthians 7:2-5).

- "The wife is bound by the law as long as her husband liveth; but if her husband be dead, she is at liberty to be married to whom she will; only in the Lord" (I Corinthians 7:39).
- "I will therefore that the younger women marry, bear children, guide the house, give none occasion to the adversary to speak reproachfully" (I Timothy 5:14).
- "Because the Lord hath been witness between thee and the wife of thy youth, against whom thou hast dealt treacherously; yet is she thy companion, and the wife of thy covenant. And did he not make one? Yet had he the residue of the spirit. And wherefore one? That he might seek a godly seed. Therefore take heed to your spirit, and let none deal treacherously against the wife of his youth" (Hebrews 13:4).
- "Marriage is honourable in all, and the bed undefiled: but whoremongers and adulterers God will judge" (Malachi 2:14-16).
- "Wives, submit yourselves unto your own husbands, as unto the Lord. For the husband is the head of the wife, even as Christ is the head of the church; and he is the saviour of the body. Therefore as the church is subject unto Christ, so let the wives be to their own husbands in every thing. Husbands, love your wives, even as Christ also loved the church, and gave himself for it" (Ephesians 5:22-25).
- "Even as Sara obeyed Abraham, calling him lord: whose daughters ye are, as long as ye do well, and are not afraid with any amazement. Likewise, ye husbands, dwell with them according to knowledge, giving honour unto the wife, as unto the weaker vessel, and as being heirs together of the grace of life; that your prayers be not hindered" (I Peter 3:6-7).

I should note that these are but a fraction of the scriptures regarding the marriage covenant. The overwhelming lesson they teach us is that marriage is a covenant between a man, a woman, and God.

Until now, laws forbidding sexual immorality were something I just took for granted. No more. They are laws of blessing, hope, self-esteem, and protection. We must teach them with logic and advocate them with reasoned argument.

We are told that the "two shall become one flesh." Husbands and wives find completeness in their lives through that which was ordained by God. The family is the bedrock of society. Ideally it should be a foundation of love, mutual respect, self-respect, sharing, and responsibility. From marriage comes our greatest gift and treasure in this world, our children and our future. The wife and husband as mother and father are by example, conversation, and action the molders of unknowing innocent children. It is not a responsibility to fear but rather an experience of joy. From the cutting of the first tooth to graduations to marriages and grandchildren, their achievements and joys, their problems and difficulties are ours.

I have often thought, as I watched my own children growing and developing, that God must see us in the same way, only greatly magnified. Having children must be one of God's greatest gifts, because the depth of love we feel for them is a reflection of the depth of love he has for us. John 3:16 tells us, "For God so loved the world, that he gave his only begotten Son, that whosoever believeth in him should not perish, but have everlasting life." There is hardly a person alive who would not give his life for his child.

Children need both parents. They need that security and completeness. Completeness of the whole, the one. The scriptures say, "provoke not your children to wrath." This doesn't mean not to discipline them. It doesn't mean that we should spoil them. What can provoke our children, though? Impatience, negative criticism, harsh language, ignoring them, not listening to them, fault-finding, intimidation, physical and mental abuse, and sexual molestation can and should provoke them, but the most common cause of anger and hurt in children today is probably divorce. In most studies I have read, children almost always blame themselves, heaping undeserved guilt upon themselves. Parents are usually the most important relationships children have until adolescence. If something goes wrong between the mother and father, the child's world is in turmoil and chaos. He is scared, fearful, riddled with anxiety, and his safe, secure world is crumbling. Wouldn't you feel anger if two grown-ups forgot the real priorities of living? If the two people responsible for teaching and nurturing you were so concerned about themselves that you got lost in the shuffle? I would be. This is not an indictment of all parents in this situation. There are circumstances that cannot be resolved. And it takes two to come to some agreement if there are difficulties in a marriage. As we shall see, there are two exits from marriage for the Christian. If the Christian is left or deserted by a non-believer, then they are free. The other exit is if one party engages in adultery.

Unfortunately, adultery is one of the primary reasons for divorce, the dissolution of the family. Why is adultery wrong? I could simply state that God said not to do it, but there are compelling reasons not to enter into this conduct.

When we marry, we take an oath before witnesses to love, cherish, and honor our spouse in sickness and health, until death do us part. Bride and groom say their vows to each other, but above all, the oath and vows are stated before God and bind us to Him. These vows of fidelity, the forsaking of all others, are the foundation of moral order for family security and trust. They give us confidence in the future and create stability in the marriage. In a larger sense, this contributes to the stability of community, state, and nation. I can be loyal to many principles and earthly powers, but the loyalty sworn to in the marriage vows supersedes all other manmade loyalties. The marriage vows are in accordance with the will of God and under His divine law.

Civil law condones the immorality that violates the marriage contract through "no-fault" divorces, euphemistically called "irreconcilable differences." How bland and feeble. Our laws are being so watered down, becoming so non-specific, that they are deceitful. It is almost as if, by changing the words, we can alter fundamental truths. No matter what accommodations civil law makes for divorce, the certain law of God stands. The laws of marriage, when perverted by man, can spell nothing but the ruin of society and nation. If the foundation of society is esteemed so little, the society has condemned itself to destruction from within, for the state *cannot* replace family bonds. Plato sought to alter this natural and spiritual law in his treatise *The Republic*. Karl Marx tried again, then the former Union of Soviet Socialist Republics, the Nazis and Adolph Hitler. All have fallen. When you pervert, alter, or nullify by civil law that which is ordained by God, you destroy the very justification for civil law.

The act of adultery destroys the one who commits it and all members of the family. Husband, wife, children, grandparents, all feel the sting of this violation. Its affects the community, the state, and the nation. The damage wreaked by divorce can have disastrous consequences. Children can be kidnapped by a parent—even murder occurs. In 1991 a man went into a courtroom, pulled a gun, murdered a judge and an attorney, wounded others, and was finally captured. All of this destruction was because he believed he had been wronged in a divorce case. If we say that the community is not affected by our personal decisions, we are only lying to ourselves. Just look at one of today's major criminal trials. Again and again we learn from the media that the defendant came from a "broken home." When we are informed of that fact, we instantly feel compassion. Why? Because we know innately that a broken home is a contradiction of what we believe and know in the depths of our hearts to be right. And we know that even when the effects are not as dramatic as in these court cases, people are damaged when families break apart.

We must strengthen families, support Godly rule of our lives, accept responsibility for our words, make a commitment to our children; we must stand firmly rooted, not giving sway to human philosophers, matters of convenience, or doing what "feels" good. "Feeling" has little to offer us when troubles come—and they do come. It is the power of the family to unite, work together, to see a problem through that gives strength to society. There is nothing finer in all the world than a man who speaks truth and honors his word. He is the man upon whom you can rely when everything and everyone is gone.

When parents divorce, no matter how fine the qualities of the parent, life becomes hard. Divorces are costly—attorneys are the only winners. And the quality of life often is lowered for one or both spouses and the children. The custodial parent is often forced to seek financial assistance from family, friends, or government welfare agencies. The custodial parent must work and is no longer able to give special attention to their child or children, attention that the young ones need and deserve. The thread and continuity of their daily lives is broken both personally and publicly. Divorce is a deep tragedy, and the weight of the tragedy is being felt in every level of society.

In several of the previous scriptures we read the word "submit."

Make no mistake, to submit is neither to be subservient nor subordinate; it means, rather, by choice and election deliberately giving recognition and authority to the husband as head of the family. In Ephesians 5, men are told three times to love their wives; women are only reminded of their responsibility twice. It is very easy for a woman to accept her husband as the head of the family when he behaves in a loving and giving way and assumes the leadership that inherently comes with the roles of husband and father. A large number of marital difficulties have their origin in the failure to abide by these principles. Adherence to them brings a good, enduring marriage whether both are believers or not.

With all there is to lose emotionally and financially, I should think that common sense would dictate communicating and correcting problems. There is so much to lose but so much more to gain. Marriage is a two-way street. We all know it, but we must be prepared at all times to give 100 percent, not 50 percent. Be ready and willing to give of yourself, your heart, your love, your forgiveness, your tenacity, and patience, so that the family will be preserved.

CHAPTER FIFTEEN

Abortion: Human By Degrees?

Abortion is legal in this country and in many others. But just because an action is legal doesn't make it moral. It has become fashionable to say, "You can't legislate morality." This is an absurd statement. What are laws but a reflection of a nation's morality, its standards, and its virtues, or lack thereof?

We have been pretending for so long that laws can exist apart from morality that many people have lost touch with their moral reactions. Perhaps the best example of this phenomenon is how people have turned off their natural moral reaction to abortion. We are understandably horrified when presented with accounts of condoned murder, such as the genocide of Jews and Gypsies by the Nazis, or the Serbs by the Croats, or the Armenians by the Turks. Pharaoh's wanton murder of the boy babies of the Hebrews evokes similar reactions, as does the gospel narrative of Herod slaughtering the innocents of Bethlehem in order to kill the Christ. If these acts disturb us, how could we possibly have become hardened to abortion, which has led to the destruction of millions of innocent lives?

One answer is that we are supposed to accept that a fetus is not yet an actual human. For convenience' sake, we are expected to regard it as a mass or group of cells. Scripture, however, presents a very different picture of the earliest moments of human life:

> For thou has possessed my reins: thou hast covered me in my

mother's womb. I will praise thee; for I am fearfully and wonderfully made: marvelous are thy works; and that my soul knoweth right well. My substance was not hid from thee, when I was made in secret, and curiously wrought in the lowest parts of the earth. Thine eyes did see my substance, yet being imperfect; and in thy book all my members were written, which in continuance were fashioned, when as yet there was none of them (Psalm 139:13-16).

This scripture reveals that a human life begins at conception, that everything the growing child will carry into adulthood is present from the beginning. Are we to believe that the fetus is a mere collection of cells one moment, and the next moment, human? If this is so, then who can tell us when that moment occurs? Or perhaps we are to assume that a human being becomes human by degrees.

We prefer to see things in "shades of gray," but the truth is that the fetus is either alive or not, and if it is alive, it is human. If we observe what happens at death, we see that the actual instance of death happens all at once. We are; or we are not. Human wishes, delusions, convenience, and ignorance cannot alter the truth.

The fact that the fetus is hidden in the womb does not make it less human. We can't see bacteria with our naked eye, but they exist. Ignorance of sterilization and hygiene doesn't stop epidemics or pandemics. We can't see bacteria, but we can see their effects. So it is with the human in the womb. We can't see it at the moment of conception, but it is already a complete human life; the passage of a few months' time will provide the evidence.

The fact that the fetus is wholly dependent on a mother for its life does not alter its human nature. Instead of projecting forward from a mass of cells to an eventual human, we should think backward, from a fully mature human to its beginning in the womb. Just think—every person who was ever born, including those we love, respect, and admire, began in the womb. Aristotle advocated this kind of reasoning. He said, "the nature of a thing is its end, or what each thing is when fully developed, we call its nature, whether we are speaking of a man, a horse, or a family. The final cause and end of a thing is the best, and to be self-sufficing, is the end and the best." Using Aristotle's logic, we can say that the unborn child's natural end is to become self-sufficient; barring any natural or unnatural interference, he will become capable of caring for his own needs and wants.

Contemporary reasoning calls the fetus a mass of cells that is not viable or self-sufficient, and therefore not human. But after a child is born, it is still not self-sufficient, and won't be for many years. Yet no one disputes that a child of, say, three years old is human and that to take its life is both unlawful and morally wrong. Here, the modern logic that condones abortion breaks down.

Aside from the fetus's status as human, we must also remember that it is already a physical body that feels pain and comfort. Evidently, doctors, nurses, and pregnant women wish to ignore the pain inflicted by the saline solution and dismembering that are part of the abortion process. Abortion may not be as dramatic as a burning at the stake or the drawing and quartering of history, but it is a torturous way to die, and it is executed on the truly innocent. The life is extinguished, but not the soul. The soul returns to God, blameless. God will not, however, hold blameless the people who shed innocent blood: "These six things doth the Lord hate: yea, seven are an abomination unto him: A proud look, a lying tongue, *and hands that shed innocent blood.* An heart that deviseth wicked imaginations, feet that be swift in running to mischief, A false witness that speaketh lies, and he that soweth discord among brethren" (Proverbs 6:16-19).

It is said over and over of abortion, "It is a woman's choice. She has power over her own body." What choice? What power? First, let's consider the matter of choice. Yes, choice is involved, but the choice begins when a woman and a man choose to have sexual intercourse. In our time, the so-called sexual revolution has made sex between consenting adults about as important and beautiful as a perfunctory handshake, with not much more excitement than a ten-minute roller coaster ride. The results can be longer and more enduring, however: a child, considered by many as nothing more than an inconvenience that can be disposed of.

As for power, of course women should have the right to make choices in life. But only God has the power to create life. We humans can create nothing. We can make, invent, discover, but we cannot create. As God tells us in Luke 12:7, "But even the hairs of our head are numbered. Fear not therefore: ye are of more value than many sparrows." In other words, we are made according to God's plan, even down to the smallest details, including the number of hairs on our heads. We have a few choices about our hair—its style and color. We can alter it a little, but we have no power to change its nature. We make choices because God gave us free will. We are not able to change the originating structure of anything. He gave us freedom with limitations. The limitations can be accepted or rejected, but when mankind tries to tamper with God's laws, the results are chaos, immorality, double meanings, and contradictions.

I have seen a television commercial/public service announcement that stated, "Children: Our greatest natural resource." This statement underscores a startling contradiction—that, ironically, in this time of extreme environmentalist thought, when people seek to protect wildlife, the earth, and the atmosphere, human life is ascribed such low value that it can be destroyed with little or no distress. Why are we turned so upside down in our thinking? It is a hideous paradox that the world is more concerned with animal rights than human rights. Some people who will not eat meat for fear of hurting an animal will without hesitation kill an unborn child in a most cruel manner.

Here is another contradiction: Two women were jailed in Texas because they were not taking proper care of their bodies during pregnancy, and women have been charged with injuring their unborn children with drugs and alcohol. Human wisdom reveals itself as foolishness through these inconsistent laws, which tell us that is perfectly all right to destroy, an unborn child, but not to injure or hurt it. Obviously, we have diametrically opposed laws on the books; these laws cannot both be morally right. If the fetus is not a living human, how can we make laws that punish a woman for doing injury to it? The only logical conclusion is that it is in fact wrong to harm a fetal human, and that abortion is legalized murder.

There is no question that manmade laws have departed from God's will with regard to abortion. Clearly, God does not approve of the killing of unborn children: "If men strive, and hurt a woman with child, so that her fruit depart from her, and yet no mischief follow: he shall be surely punished, according as the woman's husband will lay upon him; and he shall pay as the judges determine. And if any mischief follow, then thou shalt give life for life" (Exodus 21:22-25).

When we select our lawmakers, we have to know where they stand. The one burning question is, "Do they stand for the acceptance or avoidance of responsibility?" That is what the abortion question is really about, although the issues may be argued using some very lofty-sounding philosophical terms. Everything in life is a matter of balance: black/white, night/day, summer/winter, hot/cold, life/death. We cannot overlook another crucial balance: that of pleasure and responsibility. With 1.6 million abortions a year, we are hedonistically avoiding responsibility. We must wake up and accept responsibility for life, for our actions and their consequences.

One of the primary tenets of law is "Silence gives consent." When will we end our silence? When will we say, "It is wrong, it is enough, it is finished"? When will we stand, firmly rooted, and say, "No more"? Do not take part through silence. As the British statesman Edmund Burke said, "All that is necessary for evil to triumph is for good people to do nothing."

CHAPTER SIXTEEN

Rational Environmentalism

By Belinda B. Stanley
Science Chair
St. Thomas' Episcopal School

"The earth doesn't belong to man; man belongs to the earth." This statement, popular among environmental activists, directly contradicts what God says in Psalm 115:16: "The highest heavens belong to the Lord, but the earth he has given to man." When God gave man dominion over the earth, "God blessed them, and God said unto them, Be fruitful, and multiply, and replenish the earth, and subdue it; and have dominion over the fish of the sea, and over the fowl of the air, and over every living thing that moveth upon the earth" (Genesis 1:28). At this moment, after creating man in His own image, God certainly never intended for man to change it from a paradise into a desert wasteland. But then, God knew that man is capable of sin and that sin distorts everything.

In his infinite wisdom, knowing what lay ahead for the earth after man was driven forth from the Garden of Eden to work the ground, God had designed the earth in such a way that even if it were ill-used, it could heal itself. Many senior citizens remember all too well the "dust bowl" of the 1930s. Today, the prairies are again fertile and farmers of the great plains learned a valuable lesson about soil conservation. Too bad they didn't bother to read the Bible. The Israelites we commanded in ancient times to let a portion of their fields lie fallow every seventh year so that the soil might replenish itself and the poor and animals might eat what grew without cultivation:

"And six years thou shalt sow thy land, and shalt gather in the fruits thereof: But the seventh year thou shalt let it lie rest and lie still: that the poor of thy people may eat: and what they leave the beasts of the field shall eat. In like manner thou shalt deal with thy vineyard, and thy olive yard." God didn't leave us without an instruction manual!

Beginning in the early 1970s, quieting a little during the '80s, and rearing its head again in the '90s, the so-called environmental movement got underway. If truly understood, this movement can clearly be seen as yet another ploy against the American institutions of free enterprise and private property. It is the classic wolf in sheep's clothing. Of course there is something noble and morally compelling about "saving the earth." Christians are naturally drawn toward efforts to conserve natural resources and keep our environment beautiful and healthy. There is nothing wrong with this. In fact, we are commanded to "love thy neighbor as thyself," which certainly extends to not polluting each other's air, water, and soil.

It is first necessary, I believe, to understand the world view of many of today's environmental activists. While many are atheists, or more likely pantheists, a good number consider themselves deists, if not Christians. However, many of these misguided people are sold on an evolutionary view of the origin of life and our planet. This view does two things: one, it places on equal footing flora, fauna, and man; two, it causes these environmentalists to contradict themselves in their fervor to insist that man is destroying the earth.

Many people think that evolution is a new idea, that Charles Darwin thought of it in the nineteenth century, but it is mentioned in the Old Testament, in Psalm 100: "it is He that hath made us and not ourselves." Even in David's time there were men who thought that they had created themselves in the sense that there was no outside Intelligence, no Creator God, involved. The earth and everything on it "just happened." It was a series of events whose outcome was determined totally by chance. No planning, no design, no God. Some Christians concede that God may have injected some spirituality into man somewhere along his climb from ape to man but that his origin was completely mechanistic.

If one were to suppose for a moment that there is no God, then life would have to be the result of evolution. If that were true, then man is an animal, separated from other animals only by his ability to speak, write, and pass on his thoughts to the next generation. Almost everything you read about the destruction of the environment places the blame squarely on the shoulders of *Homo Sapiens.* If we were just out of the picture, there would be no pollution (our factories and cars), no global warming, no destruction of the ozone, et cetera. Basically, a lot of the environmentalist philosophy is anti-human, pure and simple. But here is where they contradict themselves; if man is an animal, if he did evolve on the same earth as the rest of the animals and plants, then he is part of the natural world and so are his cars, factories, trash dumps, and chloroflourocarbons (those bad molecules destroying the ozone layer). So how can man be set apart and accused of the impossible feat of destroying the earth?

One of the main issues that concerns environmentalists is the extinction of animal species. They have succeeded in having many aninals and even some plants placed on the "endangered species" list and protected under federal law. This has been necessary, in some cases, and has even succeeded in allowing the population of certain animals, such as the bald eagle, to regain sufficient numbers so as to no longer be in imminent danger of being lost forever.

In other situations, however, animals have been protected to the detriment of large segments of the human population in the area. A case in point would be the recent furor over the rights of the spotted owl versus those of logging companies and the many people who depend upon this industry for their livelihooods. There simply must be a commonsense solution that will allow the species to be preserved, perhaps in another, similar, habitat. Under no circumstances, however, can any sane, God-fearing person believe that man's right to harvest the trees should be sacrificed for the sake of a bird. Christians know that God is taking care of these types of situations: In Matthew 10:29, Jesus said, "Are not two sparrows sold for a farthing? And one of them will not fall to the ground apart from the will of your Father" (NIV). In verse 31, he sais, "Ye are of more worth than many sparrows." It is clear from the Scriptures that God values people more than birds. This is not clear in the environmentalist movement, wherein people are clearly not valued above other organisms. I find it interestig that most environmental activists are also pro-abortion. A cartoon I saw recently in a Christian publication showed an unborn baby whose mother was walking into an abortion clinic saying to himself, "I wish I were a whale." How true.

An interesting tenet of evolutionary thought that environmentalists never seem to mention is that countless thousands of species have become extinct over the millions of years that life has existed on the earth. Yet man has only been around for less than a million years (depending on when you want to begin to call him "man"). How, then, can we suddenly be responsible for the extinction of so many species of flora and fauna? No wonder they don't mention it.

I would be the first to deny that we human beings have been perfect or even always adequate stewards of our beautiful and bounteous earth. That, as I stated before, is the result of our sinful nature. As Christians, we need to take a leadership role in conservation and cleaning up some of our messes; as Americans, we need to set an example of stewardship for the rest of the world. But we have to be reasonable about this. No one really wants to go back to a time when there was no electricity, no cars, no telephone, no indoor plumbing, or no antibiotics. It is well known that totalitarian systems of government such as existed in the former Soviet Union are no deterrent to the destruction of the environment. This is most likely due to the fact that since nothing is privately owned, land and resources are not valued. I believe that we have the technology and the inventiveness to have both modern conveniences and maintain the ecological balance of the earth. After all, God did give us some leeway: the earth is not nearly as fragile as Al Gore and his adherents would have us to believe.

Take, for example, the so-called greenhouse effect, which is said to be responsible for a global warming trend that some scientists believe has been occurring over the last few decades. The accumulation of certain gases such as carbon dioxide and methane in the atmosphere due to increased industrial activity is said to be trapping the infrared rays (low energy radiation perceived as heat) near the surface of the earth that are normally reflected into space. The situation is exacerbated by the clear cutting of forests in many parts of the world as plants, of course, use carbon dioxide in photosynthesis to manufacture carbohydrates and give off oxygen as a byproduct. This sounds like a very reasonable hypothesis but unfortunately it is based primarily on emotional hype and not on scientific evidence.

There is no significant consensus among scientists today that global temperatures are actually increasing. How could there be?

We have at best only a couple of hundred years of temperature measurements from various places around the world, and these were hardly taken with any consistency. For example, let's say you had temperature readings from Houston's Hobby Airport every month for the last fifty years. A lot of development has occurred during that time period: more concrete roads, air strips, etc., less grass and trees. If the average temperature reading showed a gradual increase of a degree or two it would not surprise anyone!

There are two schools of thought concerning the age of the earth even among creationists. The fundamentalist group call themselves "young earth creationists" and believe the earth is less than ten thousand years old as it is recorded in Scripture. The other group, most commonly called theistic evolutionists, believes the earth is four billion years old, the age accepted by the scientific establishment. Either way you look at it, even if we had temperature readings taken with the utmost consistency since the American War for Independence, we would still be unable to make any kind of reasonable prediction about global warming and what trends it is going to follow in the next two hundred years.

Another important aspect of this debate frequently overlooked by doomsday environmentalists is the fact that volcanic eruptions like that of Mount St. Helens in 1980 produce tremendous amounts of the same kinds of gases that are emitted by industrial sources (and it was a relatively small volcano.) If you take into account the cumulative effect of all the volcanoes that have erupted since the earth's origin (whenever you take that to be) then fifty or even a hundred years' worth of industrial pollutants pales by comparison. Man can be extremely arrogant when it comes to his imagined effects upon the earth when God, who placed the earth just the right distance from the sun so that life would be possible, is left out of the formula.

A similar situation is the perceived threat to the ozone layer. Ozone is a molecule consisting of three atoms of oxygen bonded together whereas the oxygen we breathe is diatomic. Ozone is created high up in the atmosphere when high energy rays from the sun convert diatomic oxygen to ozone. Right before a thunderstorm we sometimes smell the pungent odor of ozone after lightning has contributed its energy to do the same thing near the ground. The ozone layer in the atmosphere protects us from most of the high energy rays of the sun which are known to cause some skin cancers in people and may have harmful effects on the other organisms as well. One type of pollutant produced by man which is said to be destroying the ozone layer is a group of chemicals called chlorofluorocarbons. A well-known example is the freon used in airconditioning and refrigeration. The culprit atom that destroys the ozone is chlorine. Again, the amount of chlorinereleasing compounds such as hydrochloric acid released by volcanoes dwarfs the amount of chlorofluorocarbons emitted into the atmosphere by man. Even if we gave up our airconditioners, refrigerators and hair spray (with CF propellants) it would not significantly reduce the amount of ozone being destroyed naturally, which, by the way, seems to go in cycles, not in a steadily downward trend.

A significant amount of pollution is caused by burning of fossil fuels, primarily oil, coal and natural gas. Fossil fuels, found in rock reservoirs in the ground, are thought to be the remains of prehistoric plants and animals whose hydrocarbon molecules were transformed from the carbohydrates, fats, and proteins found in living organisms into the hydrocarbon mixtures which we refine and use as fuel. Isn't this a prime example of God's amazing forethought and providence? In today's environmentalist lingo, it's recycling, pure and simple. When fossil fuels are burned efficiently, the only products are carbon dioxide and water, both of which are used by plants in photosynthesis. In the event that the amount of carbon dioxide is in excess of the amount needed by plant life, the sea can act as a reservoir for the remainder. The ocean, after all, covers threefourths of the surface of the earth, and its carbonate shell-forming animals are very numerous. Unfortunately, impurities in the hydrocarbons and inefficient burning can produce undesirable products such as sulfur dioxide and carbon monoxide. These emissions can be efficiently controlled through the use of proper technology and the enforcement of laws that are already on the books.

An alternative to the use of fossil fuels which would cut down on the rate of pollution and conserve these hydrocarbons for other uses where electricity is not practical, is the use of electrical power by means of nuclear reactors. It is only the hype and hysteria generated by the environmental activists that have slowed down the development of nuclear power plants in this country. The Chernobyl "accident" was a tragedy, but it has become clear that Soviet power plants were not built with the elaborate safeguards necessary for the prevention of disaster. This has clearly not been the case in the United States. Not one person has been killed in an American nuclear accident.

Christians *must* take a leadership role in conservation efforts where common sense and the golden rule should dictate our actions. If we ignore environmental activists, the vast majority of whom are not Christians and some of whom are most definitely anti-Christian and anti-capitalist, we are going to be in for a real doomsday, not environmental, but economic. Environmentalists have the attention and sympathy of the dominant media culture and the financial public-relations clout of Hollywood celebrities who are interested in easing their guilt about some of the movies they are making.

Religion is a necessary part of man's psychological makeup. This comes as no surprise to an adherent of God's Holy Word, the Bible. We believe that we were created by God in His image and redeemed by His only Son so that we might be reunited to Him instead of lost in our sin. Too many people today, especially those under forty who have been educated in a public-school system that has eliminated any mention of a Supreme Being from the curriculum, are clearly searching for some kind of substitute god. There is an interesting story about empty minds in the twelfth chapter of St. Matthew, verses 42-45: "When the unclean spirit is gone out of a man, he walketh through dry places, seeking rest, and findeth none. Then he saith, I will return into my house from whence I came out; and when he is come, he findeth it empty, swept and garnished. Then goeth he, and taketh with himself seven other spirits more wicked than himself, and they enter in and swell there: and the last state of that man is worse than the first. Even so shall it be also unto this wicked generation." If we empty our minds of God, what comes in to reside there will be nothing but evil spirits.

Today's secular environmentalism is fast ceasing to be secular. Searching for some type of spiritual substitute for the providential care of a Creator God, many people today are being lured into worshiping the earth itself. This type of New Age belief is sometimes referred to as the Gaia hypothesis. It is a rehash of the old Mother Earth idea, but it is even more dangerous because it masquerades as science and thus sounds very convincing. In the first Epistle of

Timothy, we are warned: "The Spirit clearly says that in later times some will abandon the faith and follow deceiving spirits and things taught by demons. Such teachings come through hypocritical liars, whose consciences have been seared with a red hot iron. They forbid people to marry and order them to abstain from certain foods, which God created to be received with thanksgiving by those who believe and who know the truth. For everything God created is good" (I Timothy 4:14, NIV).

CHAPTER SEVENTEEN

Animal Rights: Equality, or Stewardship?

"I Brake for Paws." That's one of the bumper stickers I frequently see on automobiles. I have the tendency to smart a little every time I read it. I always think, "And I don't?" Of course I do, except under special circumstances, such as wet roads, darkness, or speed. Late one night, about a mile from our gate, a high school senior swerved to miss a small nocturnal animal. This resulted in her death as well as the death of the animal she tried to protect. Her death was tragic, and the community's loss was deep. Not so with the animal—and justifiably not. Yes, we love our pets. Animals are an important part of our lives. There is nothing more pleasant to me than to sit on the porch at dusk and watch the grace and speed of the deer in the fields, to watch a little skunk beginning his nightly search for food, or late at night to hear the raccoons foraging and gathering fallen pecans. I have so many lovely creatures to watch—great herons and so many other birds, armadillos, and cattle. God said, when he finished Creation, "that it was good." Indeed it is. It is wonderful, marvelous, exhilarating, and at the same time, evidence that He is, was, and shall be.

Genesis 1:20-26 recounts the process of Creation:

> And God said, Let the waters bring forth abundantly the moving creature that hath life, and fowl that may fly above the earth in the open firmament of heaven. And God created great whales, and every

living creature that moveth, which the waters brought fourth abundantly, after their kind, and every winged fowl after his kind: and God saw that it was good. And God blessed them, saying, Be fruitful, and multiply, and fill the waters in the seas, and let fowl multiply in the earth. And the evening and the morning were the fifth day. And God said, let the earth bring forth the living creature after his kind, cattle, and creeping thing, and beast of the earth after his kind: and it was so. And God made the beast of the earth after his kind, and cattle after their kind, and every thing that creepeth upon the earth after his kind: and God saw that it was good. And God said, Let us make man in our image, after our likeness: and let them have dominion [responsible stewardship] over the fish of the sea, and over the fowl of the air, and over the cattle, and over all the earth and over every creeping thing that creepeth upon the earth.

All things were created by God, and He gave us rule over the animals, fish, and birds.

After the flood, God blessed Noah and his sons and once again gave dominion over the animals to mankind. It was at this time that the flesh of all animals (meat) was added to man's diet: "And God blessed Noah and his sons, and said unto them, Be fruitful, and multiply, and replenish the earth. And the fear of you and the dread of you shall be upon every beast of the earth, and upon every fowl of the air, upon all that moveth upon the earth, and upon all the fishes of the sea; into your hand are they delivered. Every moving thing that liveth shall be meat for you; even as the green herb have I given you all things" (Genesis 9:1-3).

Animals are not equal with us, nor can they have rights equal to those of mankind. There are five reasons. First, man is made in the image of God. The word "image" is used in Genesis 1:26 and comes from the Hebrew word *tselem*, meaning "in the likeness of." The same Hebrew word is used in Genesis 1:27 and again in Genesis 5:3: "And Adam lived 130 years, and begat a son in his own likeness, after his own image [*tselem*]." The teaching recurs in Genesis 9:6, which states, "Whoso sheddeth man's blood, by man shall his blood be shed: for in the image [*tselem*] of God made he man."

Secondly, in the same scripture, man was given "rule" over the animals, birds, and fish. The Hebrew word used is *radah*, meaning "to rule, tread down." In Hebrew there are five different words that we translate as "dominion" or "rule" in English; the others are *baal*, "to rule, possess, have, marry"; *mashal*, "to rule"; *reed*, "to rule"; *shalat*, "to be sultan." It can be readily seen that *radah* specifically denotes that man was given dominion over or rule of the animal kingdom for his use and for his welfare.

The third reason that animals are not equal to humans is enumerated in Jude 1:10: "But these speak evil of those things which they know not: but what they know naturally, as brute beasts, in those things they corrupt themselves;" and in II Peter 2:12: "But these as natural brute beasts; made to be taken and destroyed, speak evil of the things that they understand not; and shall utterly perish in their own corruption" (KJV).

Animals have *instinct*. Two other key words in these verses are "natural" and "brute." "Natural" is the translation for the Greek *phusikos*, meaning "belonging to nature." The important word is "brute," however. The Greek word used in both texts is *alogos*, signifying "without reason, speechless, irrational." It is interesting to note that the English word "brute" is a derivative of the Latin *brutus*, which means "dull and irrational." These three points direct us to one conclusion. Animals are not as man. Man has free will, can choose, make an election; animals cannot.

I have discussed in another chapter the meaning of natural law; here I will repeat, man by the nature of his being has life, intellect, and the ability to acquire property. These attributes were given by God, to be used in accordance with His will. Animals have life, but it is of a different nature. They do not have the power of reasoning nor the freedom to choose. They cannot negotiate wages, make contracts giving equal responsibility, nor buy or sell property.

Daniel 4:16 distinguishes between man and animal: "Let his [Nebuchadnezzar's] heart be changed from man's, and let a beast's heart be given unto him; and let seven times pass over him."

The word "heart" is rendered in the NIV as "mind." In the KJV, "heart" is logically rendered "mind" or "intellect"; the physical organ is not really at issue, because changing the physical heart would not have altered Nebuchadnezzar's behavior, which stemmed from a mental attitude. Further passages from Daniel give us the most graphic example that an animal does not have choice or free will. If Nebuchadnezzar's ability of mind had not been drastically changed, he would not have lived with animals nor eaten grass:

"The same hour was the thing fulfilled upon Nebuchadnezzar: and he was driven from men, and did eat grass as oxen, and his body was wet with the dew of heaven, till his hairs were grown like eagles' feathers, and his nails like birds' claws. And at the end of the days I Nebuchadnezzar lifted up mine eyes unto heaven, and mine understanding returned unto me, and I blessed the Most High, and I praised and honoured Him that liveth for ever, whose dominion is an everlasting dominion, and His kingdom is from generation to generation" (Daniel 4:33-34).

I think it should be noted here that his "understanding" was restored to Nebuchadnezzar. Animals don't have understanding. They are not made in the image of God.

The difference between man and animal in terms of their natures has been illustrated. There are two more exceedingly important differences, the soul and the flesh. Let us examine the earthly first. Genesis 1:24 tells us, "And God said, Let the earth bring forth the living creature after his kind, cattle, and creeping thing, and beast of the earth after his kind: and it was so." Animals come from the earth.

Earlier we have seen that God made man in His image. This was a special act. He did not bring him forth from the earth by command as he did the creatures of the earth, but actually formed him from the dust of the earth. "And the Lord God formed man of the dust of the ground, and breathed into his nostrils the breath of life; and man became a living soul" (Genesis 2:7).

The cardinal difference between man and animal is not that which can be seen, but that which is unseen: the soul. The most beautiful scripture describing the act of creation is contained here— "and breathed into his nostrils the breath of life, and man became a living soul." Mankind was special; it was the crowning glory of all of creation that our souls were given by Him and belong to Him. Ecclesiastes 3:21 states, "Who knoweth the spirit of man that goeth upward, and the spirit of the beast that goeth downward to the earth?" The spirits of the animals go back to the earth and man's spirit goes back to God. Ecclesiastes 12:7: "Then shall the dust return to earth as it was: and the spirit shall return unto God who gave it." We know that although our bodies return to dust, our spirits go home to Him. We have a new life, a new body. Philippians 3:21: "Who shall change our vile body, that it may be fashioned like unto his glorious body, according to the working whereby he is able even to subdue all things unto himself." I Cornithians 15:42-44: "So also is the resurrection of the dead. It is sown in corruption, it is raised in incorruption: It is sown in dishonor, it is raised in glory: It is sown in weakness, it is raised in power: It is sown a natural body; and it is raised a spiritual body."

Another difference between man and animals is the flesh. I Corinthians 15:39 states, "All flesh is not the same flesh: but there is one kind of flesh of beasts, another of fishes, and another of birds." Man and animal are different even in that point. We are different in spirit, mind, and flesh. We have no equality except that the Lord cares for all of His creation and takes care of it all. Matthew 6:26 reminds us, "Behold the fowls of the air: for they sow not, neither do they reap, nor gather into barns; yet your heavenly Father feedeth them. Are ye not much better than they?" Here is God's enunciation of our superiority to the animal kingdom.

Since God in His wisdom gave us dominion and rule over the animal kingdom, we must examine some of the rules that He gave to guide us. "And the fear of you and the dread of you shall be upon every beast of the earth, and upon every fowl of the air, upon all that moveth upon the earth, and upon all the fishes of the sea; into your hand are they delivered. Every moving thing that liveth shall be meat for you; even as the green herb have I given you all things. But flesh with the life thereof, which is the blood thereof, shall ye not eat" (Genesis 9:2-4).

Yes, we may eat meat, poultry, and fish. Under the Mosaic Law there were restrictions. They were removed at the resurrection of the Christ, the Law having been fulfilled. Romans 6:14 puts it this way: "For ye are not under the law, but under grace." Christ verifies in Matthew 25:35, "For I was hungered and ye gave me meat." Luke said in Acts 2:46 "And they, continuing daily with one accord in the temple, and breaking bread from house to house, did eat their meat with gladness and singleness of heart." In Acts 27:33 we read, "And while the day was coming on, Paul besought them all to take meat, saying, This day is the fourteenth day that ye have tarried and continued fasting, having taken nothing." Christ in Luke 15:27 said, "Thy father hath killed the fatted calf."

Again and again we have confirmation of meat as an acceptable food. We even have affirmation through a warning. Paul tells us in I

Timothy 4:3: "Forbidding to marry, and commanding to abstain from meats, which God hath created to be received with thanksgiving of them which believe and know the truth."

Our responsibility, then, is to have an attitude of appreciation for His gifts and to fulfill our role as stewards of those gifts. To refuse meat because you don't want it is one thing, but to refuse it because of manmade constraint is unlawful, whether it be due to civil law or supposedly religious doctrine. That which God has called good is not to be disdained. Do we know better than the Creator? The Creator has given us the plants, herbs, and animals for our good and to the benefit of our bodies.

With dominion and rule also come responsibility, and we do have examples about our care of animals. I Timothy 5:18 tells us, "For the scripture saith, Thou shall not muzzle the ox that treadeth out the corn. And, The labourer is worthy of his reward."

We must feed animals. We must shelter them when there is need, as told us by example in Genesis 33:17: "And Jacob journeyed to Succoth, and built him a house, and made booths for his cattle: therefore the name of the place is called Succoth." In Genesis 6:19-21 we learn, "And of every living thing of all flesh, two of every sort shalt thou bring into the ark, to keep them alive with thee; they shall be male and female. Of fowls after their kind; two of every sort shall come unto thee, to keep them alive. And take thou unto thee of all food that is eaten, and thou shalt gather it to thee; and it shall be for food for thee, and for them." We see that God directed Noah to shelter and feed all the animals that were taken into the Ark.

One of the most simply stated examples of caring for animals is contained in the Gospels of Luke, 2:7-8: "And she brought forth her firstborn son, and wrapped him in swaddling clothes, and laid him in a manger; because there was no room for them in the inn, And there were in the same country shepherds abiding in the field, keeping watch over their flock by night." Our Savior was born in a stable and shepherds were in the fields caring for their sheep.

Working from God's word, there are examples to be followed, and if we own animals, there is common sense to be exercised, too. If I had a mule that pulled a plow, I wouldn't beat it or cut its hamstring, because that would render the animal useless, incapable of doing his work. In the example of the ox, how could he work if he were starved? Animals are useful and necessary for us. If you have a beautiful rosebush, you aren't going to deny it water and fertilizer or allow it to freeze in winter. Why would you deny an animal such things? You wouldn't. Proverbs 12:10 states, "A righteous man cares for the needs of his animal" (NIV).

Genesis 10:8-9 tells us of Nimrod: "And Cush begat Nimrod: he began to be a mighty one in the earth. He was a mighty hunter before the Lord: wherefore it is said, Even as Nimrod the mighty hunter before the Lord." Genesis 27:3-5 speaks of Esau, "Now therefore take, I pray thee, thy weapons, thy quiver and thy bow, and go out to the field, and take me some venison; And make me savoury meat, such as I love, and bring it to me, that I may eat; that my soul may bless thee before I die."

Both were hunters. We are not told what Nimrod hunted, but it was with God's approval, as shown by the statement, "before the Lord." In Esau's case, we know that Isaac loved tasty meat and from the scriptures we can discern that Esau must have hunted often so that his father could have his favorite food.

The Bible is full of examples of animals being used for labor. We read above of the ox in Deuteronomy 25:4. Genesis 45:17 offers, "And Pharaoh said unto Joseph, Say unto thy brethren, This do ye; lade your beasts, and go, get you unto the land of Canaan." Oxen were used to carry loads, pull tools, mill grains, and pull sleds. They were a means of survival. Other animals are used in a similar fashion. My mother-in-law always had canaries in her home. They served as a warning for gas leaks before odor additives were included in the natural gas. Miners took canaries into the mines. In both instances, if the canaries suddenly died, they knew there was danger from gas.

Leviticus 24:21 states, "And he that killeth a beast, he shall restore it: and he that killeth a man, he shall be put to death." Genesis 31:41 says, "I have served six years for thy cattle": they are property to be earned. These two scriptures show the relationship of God to man and animals to man.

In God's eyes and under His laws, we can replace an animal, for as earlier shown, they are under our dominion and rule. Man is under the dominion and rule of God, and we answer to Him for killing man. Genesis 9:5: "And surely your blood of your lives will I require; at the hand of every beast will I require it, and at the hand of man; at the hand of every man's brother will I require the life of man." In the scripture, the taking a of man's life is placed under God's dominion, for if animals or man kill man, God will punish. Man is not under the injunction for killing animals. Man has his place, and animals have theirs. In Psalm 8:5 we learn man's place: "For thou has made him a little lower than the angels, and hast crowned him with glory and honour."

Do not be inclined toward modern philosophies, for they are nothing but a reflection of paganism; a case of worshipping the created rather than the Creator, as described in Romans 1:25: "Who changed the truth of God into a lie, and worshipped and served the creature more than the Creator, who is blessed for ever."

When we violate God's order in nature and give respect when it is not due, give worth that God has not, we pervert the Word. Many people today believe that the animal kingdom is of a higher order than God created it. Romans 9:20-21 makes the animal's place clear: "Nay but, O man, who art thou that repliest against God? Shall the thing formed say to him that formed it, Why hast thou made me thus? Hath not the potter power over the clay, of the same lump to make one vessel unto honour, and another unto dishonour?" We are the clay; the animals are also clay. One has honor, the other does not. One is made in His image; the other is not. No matter who speaks differently, animals are not equal to man. This natural law will not and cannot be altered. God is constant and consistent. He is the same yesterday, today, and tomorrow. Our places on earth were established at the Creation. It hasn't changed and will not change in the future. Remember II Timothy 4:3-4: "For the time will come when they will not endure sound doctrine; but after their own lusts shall they heap to themselves teachers, having itching ears; from the truth, and shall be turned unto fables." Don't be seduced by gentle and kind-sounding fables. Test them against the Word: It is the Rock upon which all truth is based; a guide for living in a modern world, both secularly and spiritually.

CHAPTER EIGHTEEN

The Ripple In the Pond

To preserve and protect—this is the function of government. Increasingly, though, since the 1930s, government has moved beyond the bounds of this purpose. It has sought to structure, regulate, perfect, and mold our national character in a "politically correct" image. Political correctness is a sham, a manmade ideal attempting to replace the true image that should be emulated.

Any manmade ideal is a poor substitute for the original, natural pattern. Mankind would never even dream of attempting to make a better robin. Why do we then have the arrogance to think that we can mold a better society by following a manmade prescription instead of a natural, Godly one? In chapter seven, we learned how secular humanism holds that good and bad are discerned solely through experience. It is safe to suggest that experience has taught us but one thing: We humans don't comprehend good and evil by our own understanding. The present condition of our society proves our lack of comprehension. At the beginning of the twenty-first century, we have traveled the road from internal discipline to externally imposed discipline with hardly a whimper, led by the crumbs of government-imposed morality, subsidies, entitlements, and a myriad of promises. We are a living contradiction to evolution theory. We have devolved from orderly, respectful people with self-imposed constraint to a nation of people whose daily lives are ruled by crime and insecurity. Our society has deposed good old-fashioned natural morality, and we will inherit the results. As de Toqueville said of Americans, we were "great because we were good, and that greatness would cease when we ceased to be good, or moral."

The causes of this decline are multiple. Educators, governmental policies, the entertainment industry, marital dissolution, and complacency have all had their part in the weaving of today's problems. It is going to require many individuals working separately and together to unravel the current fabric and restore the original for the sake of our posterity. The changes that have occurred and tilted our nation against its founding virtues did not come as an onrushing wall of floodwaters, but rather as a slow, insidious rising tide that threatens to cut us off from high ground. We cannot afford the luxury of complacency. We must recognize that there is open hostility to all religions at every level of society. To openly base your actions, beliefs, or opinions on religious convictions invites jeers, ridicule, and scorn, and your credibility is thrown on the ash heap of human wisdom. All that is needed to overcome this obstacle, however, is faith.

In the thirteenth and fourteenth chapters of Numbers, all the spies, save Caleb and Joshua, believed that the land of Canaan could not be taken by the children of Israel. Those spies had no faith in God, and no faith in their own ability when under His guidance. Lack of faith cost that rebellious generation entry into the promised land. Let us be a willing generation. It will take work, strength, perseverance, faith, and commitment. Let us not view moral decay as evidence of defeat, as the majority of Israelites did. Instead we must see it as a challenge, a victory that we can and will win for our children and grandchildren. The restoration of the nation's moral fiber is the greatest legacy that we can leave them.

Envision for a moment the Giant Sequoia trees of the West. Think about their great beauty and majesty stretching and reaching for the sunlight. How often, when viewing a majestic tree, do we think about the roots? Roots stabilize the tree and provide its sustenance. Without deep roots, the tree would wither and die. We live in a great society, and its constitution, its government, are like the trunk and branches of a mighty Sequoia. Just as those majestic trees shelter the forest floor, so our constitution shelters us. Where are the roots? The history of the colonies, their hardships and devotion to religious freedom and the freedom to pursue life, liberty, and happiness are the roots and bedrock of our constitution. Without its foundation, the constitution, too, can wither and die. That document is kept alive by the nourishment of truth, responsibility, self-discipline, industriousness, accountability, and respect for moral authority.

There was a young man in Luke 15:11-32 who came to appreciate the nourishment of a moral and responsible life. Unfortunately, he went through harrowing times to come to that appreciation. He took his inheritance and wasted it on the so-called good life. He ultimately tended swine and ate their leftovers. Finally, he remembered the condition of his father's servants' home and went there seeking only to work as a servant. He pronounced his unworthiness and said he had *sinned against heaven and his father;* by acknowledging this, he was received into his father's household and all its attendant blessings were again his.

Our nation is like the prodigal son. We've been enjoying the "good life" with no thought for the future. The solution to our difficulties is to repent our ways as a nation and return to the rational policies of the past. I know that one of the first objections to cross your mind is that "conditions change." Yes, they do. Today we have drought and tomorrow we may have flood; when the Soviet Union was our principle adversary, we had world stability and focus. Now that the U.S.S.R. has broken apart, we have a great deal of instability. Conditions change.

It is said that we can still depend on "death and taxes." We can also still depend on human nature. It doesn't change. That's where principles, moral teaching, ethics, the "right rule" of law, and the grace of a forgiving God come into the picture. They offer something to fall back on, although they should never have been forsaken. When we are tossed about as in a boat on a stormy sea, they are our compass and our rudder; they bring us safely into port, where we can lower our anchor and ride out the storm.

Just as natural law doesn't change, neither do the natural laws of society among mankind. Spiritual law doesn't change, either. Acts 17:28-31 says, "For in Him we live, and move, and have our being; as certain also of your own poets [Greeks] have said, For we are also his offspring. Forasmuch then as we are the offspring of God, we ought not to think that the Godhead is like unto gold, or silver, or stone, graven by art and man's device. *And the times of this ignorance God winked at; but now commandeth all men every where to repent:* because he hath appointed a day, in which he will judge the world in righteousness by that man whom he hath ordained; whereof he hath given assurance unto all men, in that he hath raised him from the dead."

Christ uses the analogy of natural law to explain the importance of adhering to spiritual law in Luke 6:47-49: "Whomsoever cometh to me, and heareth my sayings, and doeth them I will shew you to whom he is like: He is like a man which built an house, and digged deep, and laid the foundation on a rock: and when the flood arose, the stream beat vehemently upon a rock. But he that heareth, and doeth not, is like a man that without a foundation built an house upon the earth; against which the stream did beat vehemently and immediately it fell; and the ruin of that house, and could not shake it: for it was founded upon a rock. But he that heareth, and doeth not, is like a man that without a foundation built an house upon the earth; against which the stream did beat vehemently and immediately it fell; and the ruin of that house was great." In modern times, we have seen what happens to a nation when its foundation is not built upon a rock of truth and understanding of laws. In August 1991, on a Sunday night, the first bulletins flashed that a coup d'etat was taking place in the Soviet Union. Over the years, they had seemed to be the most formidable empire in the modern world, solid and imposing and far from collapse. I never thought to see the fall in my lifetime. I had been equally amazed to see the whisking away of the Berlin Wall practically overnight, a couple of years before. The "stream" did beat and the fall was "great," and old countries were reestablished, practically in the blink of an eye. The point is this, we think, mistakenly, that life and affairs will just continue along unchecked, that the reaping of what we are sowing will be forever delayed. The day of reckoning will come, however. If our moral standards continue to erode, if our elected officials don't accept moral responsibility for the offices they hold, if those in positions of leadership continue to be more interested in "political correctness" than in moral correctness, and most importantly, if we as citizens either wink at or wear blinders about the moral culpability of those whom we elect to public office, the fall of this nation will also be great. We must imitate the prodigal son and renew our minds and our mindset: "Finally brethren, whatsoever things are just, whatsoever things are pure, whatsoever things are lovely, whatsoever things are of good report: if there be any virtue, and if there be any praise, think on these things" (Philippians 4:8).

Everyone, everywhere needs to start a renewal of thought that will give rise to deeds and actions that will begin the process of our rebirth as a people and a nation. Our children are the future, and we need to start with ourselves in order to plant the seed for the next generation. Children imitate what they see and hear.

Children also use the tools and information we give them, even if doing so leads to their destruction. Take the following example. If I were to give a ten-year-old a car and the keys to the car and left, do you honestly think that the child would just sit on the front porch and look at it? Of course not. The first time I was out of sight, the experimenting would begin. If I gave him the needed information to operate the car, it would only fuel his determination to use what he had been given. Sex education at an early age and condom distribution in schools, violence and immorality on television, destructive song lyrics, vulgar language, and preoccupation with sex in the film industry are prime examples of giving children the keys to something they're not meant to have. We need to exercise some old-fashioned common sense and quit placing our children in harm's way. Placing them in untenable positions is going to cause them a great deal of grief and many will be burned badly if we don't stand against, what I want to believe, are well meaning, but misguided individuals and their policies. Good intentions don't always produce good results but good moral instruction does succeed when nothing else will.

When we think of the entertainment and information industries, we usually visualize great faceless behemoths, impregnable and irresistible. Nothing could be further from the truth. They are run by human beings like you and me, and because of that they can be persuaded to do what is decent and good. We just have to get busy and do some persuading. That's exactly what Dr. Richard Neill of Fort Worth, Texas, did.

Here is an example we can follow. Dr. Neill said that he never watched much television in the first place, but after the birth of his daughter in 1986, he lost his apathy. He realized that what he turned off in disgust might be viewed by his children when he and his wife weren't home to monitor them. After seeing the different offerings on "Donahue," he realized how it could affect children and decided that something had to be done. His goals were very modest and yet, for a lone individual, huge. First he got 9,000 signatures on a petition to move the program to a late-night hour. The television station did not respond. A new approach had to be tried. Neill started documenting what the shows featured, recording it on videotape and ordering transcripts. He wanted absolute truthfulness, no innuendoes, only facts. He stressed, "There is no need to exaggerate. Truth is enough."[1] His new goal was to get four sponsors to reject "Donahue." At last count it was over 100. How did Dr. Neill achieve his goal? It was really very simple and required only his tenacity. He mailed certified letters to the top executive officers and particularly to the chief executive officers of the companies advertising on the program. They seem to take more note when several letters arrive at the same time. The Sara Lee Company spokesman in Chicago said, "He stuck to the facts and helped the company. He zeroed in right away on the product involved and was straightforward and sincere. Emotional letters are not effective."[2] Dr. Neill even received a letter from Circuit City that concluded, "I applaud your willingness to get involved, and it certainly appears that your efforts are making a difference."[3] Just think what could be accomplished if in every city and town across America, just one person followed Dr. Neill's example and wrote letters about just one offensive program. Whether it is gay "marriages" being performed by gay ministers, male and female strippers, or skinheads, we don't need them on daytime television. The many latch-key children in our nation today don't need it.

There is a lot to be thankful for in this moral and cultural battle. We are not alone. There are many people and organizations out there, working, writing, talking, lobbying, and educating. We must join in and do our part. The first and most important thing we must do is hold fast to our principles and forget about being "politically correct." We must be more concerned with being right in the eyes of God, doing what is virtuous, and not worrying about the outcome. If we do what is right, He will take care of the rest in His time, not ours. If we will plant the seed, He will give the harvest, but we must plant the seed; we must be active workers. It is our right and privilege as citizens of this country, and most importantly it is our duty to God and our country to stand and be counted.

Don't for one minute let people tell you that this nation has already gone down the drain. We have not. This is still the "home of the brave and the land of the free." When France fell in 1941, Marshal Henri Petain said, "Our spirit of enjoyment was stronger than our spirit of sacrifice. We wanted to have more than we wanted to give. We tried to spare effort, and met disaster." Let that never be said of us. There are many across this nation, working separately and independently without knowledge of each other. Know that you are not alone. The signal fires are lit. All that is required is our effort to carry the torch.

Epilogue

As this book comes to completion, the turmoil of the world is increasing, and peace as the world envisions it is nowhere in sight. Our nation seems to be moving further and further away from the logic of natural law and the hope of spiritual law as revealed in the Word of God. It is my sincere prayer that our national leaders will return to policies that are in agreement with our orderly universe as created by almighty God and as observed and witnessed by the ancient philosophers and the prophets of God. Until the people of the world are willing to accept the reality and omnipotence of God, the turmoil will be unending.

The only thing that we can control is ourselves. We must shine as a light into a world of darkness and never place our ultimate hopes on any worldly power. Our hope lies in the risen Savior. We must continue to speak out and peaceably show by example a better way of life. We must follow the example of the first-century Christians and live orderly lives and take no part in acts of civil disobedience. We are to love one another, obey the law, and give no one the opportunity to point to us with accusations of corruptness. Each of us must do what he does best. Take joy in our work, love and instruct our children, and hold our heads high—but with meekness. We must stand and persevere; in doing so, we will never give comfort to any enemy. The Lord will take care of the rest.

Therefore sent he thither horses, and chariots, and a great host: and they came by night, and compassed the city about.

And when the servant of the man of God was risen early, and gone forth, behold, an host compassed the city both with horses and chariots. And his servant said to him, Alas my master! how shall we do?

And he answered, Fear not; for they that be with us are more than they that be with them.

And Elisha prayed, and said, Lord, I pray thee, open his eyes, that he may see.

And the Lord opened the eyes of the young man; and he saw: and, behold, the mountain was full of horses and chariots of fire round about Elisha.

II KINGS 6:14-17

For we wrestle not against flesh and blood, but against principalities, against powers, against the rulers of darkness of this world, against spiritul wickedness in high places.

Wherefore take unto you the whole armour of God, That ye may be able to withstand in the evil day, and having done all, to stand.

EPHESIANS 6:12-13

Endnotes

Preface
1. *The Reasonableness of Christianity*, John Locke, London, 1714 ed. *Christian History of the Constitution* (CHOC).
2. "Americanism—A Heritage of the Ages," Hon. Fritz G. Lanham, U.S. House of Representatives, Feb. 27, 1939.
3. Ephesians 6:10-17.

Chapter One
1. Plato, *Timaeus*.
2. Marcus Tullis Cicero, *De Re Publica (The Republic)*, book 3, paragraph 22.—*De Re Publica, De Legibus,* trans. Clinton W. Keys, p 211 (1943).
3. Wm. Blackstone's "Commentaries," 1765; ed. Jones, 1915, CHOC, p 141
4. Ibid.
5. Acts 17:22-31

Chapter Two
1. Aristotle, *Politics*, Book I, Chap. 2
2. Ibid

Chapter Three
1. Christian History of the U.S., Christian Self-Government, p. 28B
2. CHOC, p. 28B.

3. "The Sanctity of Law," John W. Burgess, Boston, 1927 (CHOC).
4. CHOC, p. 192.

Chapter Four
1. *Saints and Strangers*, George F. Willison, New York, Reynal & Hitchcock, 1945, p.8
2. Ibid.
3. "Genesis of the New England Churches," 1874, CHOC, p. 22
4. Ibid., p. 22
5. *Saints and Strangers*, p. 24
6. Ibid.
7. "Genesis of the New England Churches," p. 25
8. *Saints and Strangers*, George F. Willison.
9. Ibid.
10. CHOC p. 24 "Genesis"; Robert Browne published *A Treatise of Reformation without Tarrying for Anie* and *A Book which Sheweth the Life and Manner of all True Christians. 1582*, according to Geo. Willison., p.31, Middleburg, Holland
11. *Saints and Strangers*, p. 13
12. Ibid.
13. *Politics*, book VII.
14. *Expository Dictionary of N.T. Words*, Fleming H. Revell Co., 1966.
15. *Edinburgh Characters*, Michael T.R.B. Turnbull.
16. Ibid.
17. *History of the First Church in Hartford, 1633-1883*, by George Leon Walker, 1884, CHOC.
18. Beginnings of New England, 1889, John Fiske, CHOC.
19. "An Essay Concerning Human Understanding," printed by William Fessenden, Brattleboro, Vermont, 1806, second American edition.
20. Locke, *Treatise on Civil Government*, chapter XV, para. 171.

Chapter Five
1. CHOC, pp. 340–47.
2. *History of the United States*, George Bancroft, 1850.
3. *The Rights of the British Colonies Asserted and Proved*, James Otis, Boston, 1764.
5. *The American Revolution*, John Fiske.

6. *Life of Joseph Warren,* Richard Frothingham, 1865.

Chapter Six
1. *Das Kapital,* Chap.I
2. Ibid, XXIV
3. *Theory:* contemplation, speculation. A formulation of apparent relationships or underlying principles of certain observed phenomena (theory of evolution).*Webster's New World Dictionary of the American Language,* The World Publishing Co., New York, 1955.
4. *Apes, Angels and Victorians,* Julian Huxley and H.B.D. Kettlewell, McGraw Hill, 1955, p. 109
5. *Descent of Man,* Charles Darwin, Part III, Chapter XXI
6. A Sanskrit symbol.
7. *Aryan:* sans. arya, lord, master, arya, a tribal name; akin to Oper. ariya, a tribal name; orig. applicable only to the Indo-Iranian tribes, but popularized in a wider sense by Max Muller and less reputable authors; not connected with Eire, Ireland, Irish. Formerly, designating or of the family of languages that includes Iranian, Sanskrit, and most of the European languages; Indo-European. A descendant of, the prehistoric people who spoke this language. Aryan has no validity as a racial term, although it has been so used, notoriously by the Nazis to mean "a Caucasian of non-Jewish descent." *Webster's New World Dictionary.*
8. *The Occult and the Third Reich: The Mystical Origins of Nazism and the Search for the Holy Grail.* Jean-Michael Angebert, translated by Lewis A. M. Sumberg, McGraw Hill, 1974, page 169.
9. Ibid, p. 53.

Chapter Seven
1. Attributed to Alexis De Tocqueville by Dwight D. Eisenhower in his final campaign address in Boston, Massachusetts, November 3, 1952. Unverified. The last two sentences are attributed to de Tocqueville's *Democracy in America,* by Sherwood Eddy, in *The Kingdom of God and the American Dream,* 1941, p. 6. This appears with minor variations in *A Third Treasury of the Familiar,* ed. Ralph L. Woods, p. 347, 1970, as "attributed to de Tocqueville but not found in his works."
2. Simon and Schuster, 1987, p. 31.
3. *Treatise on Common Good,* chapter VI, para. 56
4. Clarence Darrow defended John Scopes, 1925, for teaching evolution ("Scopes Monkey Trial").

5. Eugene B. Debs was Socialist Party candidate for president five times, 1900-1920. Debs was heavily influenced by the works of Karl Marx, and he was highly critical of political and economic traditions, especially capitalism. Debs, who was imprisoned twice, established the Socialist Party of America in 1898.
6. John Howland Snow, *Turning of the Tides*, New Canaan, Conn: Long House, 1956.
7. Ibid.
8. *The Collected Works of Abraham Lincoln*, Roy Basler, ed., 1953, vol. 6, p. 156.
9. The Supreme Court at October Term, 1962, United States Reports, vol. 374

Chapter Nine
1. *The Law*, Frederic Bastiat, Trans. Dean Russell, The Foundation For Economic Education, Inc., 1981, Irvington-On-Hudson, NY.
2. Ibid.
3. Edmund Burke, eighteenth-century English statesman.

Chapter Ten
1. *Property*, 1792.
2. Ibid., chapter V.
3. Ibid., chapter II, p. 6.

Chapter Eleven *(there are two #3s in the text)*
1. Dean Russell, trans., The Foundation For Economic Education. Inc. Irvington-On-Hudson. N.Y., 1981, 2. Ibid.
3. Ibid.
4. *Life of Samuel Adams*, W. V. Well, 1865.
5. Locke, *Of Civil Government*, chapter XI, para. 135.
6. *The Pulpit of the American Revolution*, J. Wingate Thornton, 1860.

Chapter Twelve
1. Reprinted with permission of Dr. F. W. Mattox
2. Summary prepared by Dr. F. W. Mattox, Harding College
3. Ibid.
4. 1901 edition.
5. Ibid.
6. From the papers of Paul R. Pearce, ca. 1950

162

7. Ibid.
8. "Economic Scene," February 18, 1993.
9. *Economics in One Easy Lesson,* Henry Hazlitt, 1979

Chapter Thirteen
1. Locke, Treatise, Chapter II, p. 4.
2. Joyce Price, *The Washington Times,* December 18, 1991.

Chapter Eighteen
1. "The Quiet Man Who Tripped Up Donahue," *Citizen,* November 16, 1992, Colorado Springs, Co.
2. Ibid.
3. Ibid.

Bibliography

Ahlstrom, Sydney E. *Religious History of the American People.* New Haven: Yale Univ. Press, 1972.

Anderson, Bernhard W. "Creation." In *The Interpreter's Dictionary of the Bible.* New York and Nashville: Abingdon, 1962.

Angebert, Jean-Michel. *The Occult and the Third Reich: The Mystical Origins of Nazism and the Search for the Holy Grail.* Trans. by Lewis A. M. Sumberg. New York: McGraw Hill, 1975.

Bastiat, Frederic. *The Law.* Trans. by Dean Russell. Irvington-on-Hudson, New York: Foundation for Economic Education, 1987.

———. *Taxes.* Trans. by Dean Russell. Irvington-on-Hudson, New York: Foundation for Economic Education, 1987.

Bendersky, Joseph W. *A History of Nazi Germany.* Chicago, Ill.: Nelson-Hall, 1985

Bible Science News, P.O. Box 33220, Minneapolis, MN, 55433-0220.

Bloom, Allan. *The Closing of the American Mind: How Higher Education Has Failed Democracy and Impoverished the Souls of Today's Students.* New York: Simon and Schuster, 1987.

Burgess, John W. *The Sanctity of Law.* Boston, 1927. In Hall, Verna M., *The Christian History of the Constitution of the United States of America.* (*See* Hall, Verna M.)

Clark, Fred G., and Richard Stanton Rimanoczy. *How We Live.* Cleveland, Ohio: American Economic Foundation, 1988.

"The Implications of Federal Aid to and Control of Education." Hon. Ralph W. Gwinn, New York, remarks of. Congressional Record, 80th Congress, First Session.

Darwin, Charles. *The Descent of Man*. Encyclopaedia Britannica.

Documents of the Formation of the Union of the American States. Government Printing Office, 1927.

Eddy, Sherwood. *The Kingdom of God and the American Dream: The Religious and Secular Ideas of American History*. New York and London: Harper and Brothers, 1941.

Figgie, Harry E. *Bankruptcy 1995*. New York: Little, Brown, 1992.

Glaser, Hermann. *The Cultural Roots of National Socialism*. Trans. by Ernest A. Menze. Austin: Univ. of Texas Press, 1978.

Gore, Albert. *Earth in the Balance: Ecology and the Human Spirit*. Boston: Houghton Mifflin, 1992.

Greaves, Bettina Bien. *Free Market Economics: A Basic Reader*. Irvington-on-Hudson, New York: Foundation for Economic Education, 1984.

Hall, Verna M., comp. *The Christian History of the Constitution of the United States of America: Christian Self-Government*. San Francisco: Foundation for American Christian Education, 1987.

———. *The Christian History of the Constitution of the United States of America: Christian Self-Government with Union*. San Francisco: Foundation for American Christian Education, 1987.

———. *The Christian History of the American Revolution: Consider and Ponder*. San Francisco: Foundation for American Christian Education, 1988.

———. *The Christian History of the American Constitution: William Blackstone's Commentaries, 1765*. San Francisco: Foundation for American Christian Education.

———. *The Christian History of the American Constitution: Genesis of the New England Churches*.

Hazlitt, Henry. *Economics in One Easy Lesson*. Westport, Conn.: Arlington House, 1979.

Huxley, Julian, introd. to Chandrasekhar, Sripati, *Population and Planned Parenthood in India*. London: Allen and Unwin, 1955.

———— and H. B. D. Kettlewell. *Apes, Angels, and Victorians.* New York: McGraw Hill, 1955.

———— and ————. *Charles Darwin and His World.* New York: Viking, 1965.

Ingram, T. Robert. *New Liturgy, Old Heresy.* St. Thomas Press, 1981.

Historical Highlights of Birth Control. International Planned Parenthood Federation.

Irvine, Wlliam. *Apes, Angels, and Victorians: The Story of Darwin, Huxley, and Evolution.* New York: McGraw Hill, 1955.

Ivimy, John. *The Sphinx and the Megaliths.* New York: Harper and Row, 1975.

Johnson, Phillip E. *Darwin on Trial.* Downers Grove, Ill.: Intervarsity Press, 1991.

Lorant, Stefan. *Sieg Heil: An Illustrated History of Germany from Bismarck to Hitler.* New York: W. W. Norton, 1974.

Locke, John. *Of Civil Government.*

————. *The Reasonableness of Christianity.*

————. *Treatise on the Common Good.*

Marx, Karl. *Das Kapital.*

Methvin, Eugene. "Let Us Pray." *Reader's Digest,* November 1992.

Pagels, Elaine. *The Gnostic Gospels.* New York: Vintage Books, 1981.

Plato. *The Republic.* Encyclopaedia Britannica, 1952.

Price, Joyce, in *The Washinqton Times,* 12-18-91.

Ray, Dixy Lee, and Lou Guzzo. *Trashing the Planet: How Science Can Help Us Deal with Acid Rain, Depletion of the Ozone, and Nuclear Waste (Among Other Things).* Washington, D.C.: Regnery Gateway, 1990.

Slater, Rosalie J. *American Dictionary of the Enqlish Lanuage,* Irvington-On-Hudson, New York: Iverson Norman Assoc. Reprint of 1828 edition by G. & C. Merriam Co.

————. *Teaching and Learning America's Christian History: The Principle Approach.* San Francisco: Foundation For American Christian Education, 1992.

Snow, John Howland. *Turning of the Tides.* New Canaan, Conn.: Long House, 1956.

Thornton, J. Wingate. *The Pulpit of the American Revolution*. Boston, 1860.

Toland, John *Adolph Hitler*. New York: Doubleday, 1976.

Tocqueville, Alexis de. *Democracy in America*. In Eddy, Sherwood, *The Kingdom of God and the American Dream*. (*See* Eddy, Sherwood.)

Turnbull, Michael T. R. B. *Edinburgh Characters*. Edinburg: St. Andrew Press, 1992.

Upshur, Abel. *The Federal Government: Its Nature and Character*. Reprinted by St. Thomas Press.

Vine, W. E., and M. A. Fleming. *An Expository Dictionary of New Testament Words*. H. Revell & Co., 1966.

Wurmbrand, Richard. *Marx and Satan*. Westchester, Ill.: Crossway Books, 1986.

Wells, W. V., *The Life of Samuel Adams*, 1865.

Willison, George F. *Saints and Strangers*. New York: Reynal & Hitchcock, 1945

Young, Robert, L.L.D. *Analytical Concordance To The Bible*. Grand Rapids, Michigan: Wm. E. Eerdman Publishing Co., 1975.

Index

Abington School District v. Schempp, 69-70
abortion, 128-132
Abraham, 10, 12, 46, 79
Adam, 10, 12
Adams, John, 38
Adams, Samuel, 36-37, 96
adultery, 126
Agricultural Adjustment Act, 105
AIDS, 118-119
American Economic Foundation, 107
American Revolution, 32-42
ancient Rome, 16-18
Angebert, Jean-Michel, 54
animal rights, 141-148
Apes, Angels, and Victorians, 51
Aristotle, 10, 12-13, 15, 24
Articles of Confederation, 40
Aryans, 53
Ashley, Lord, 27
Atlantis, 53
Attlee, Clement, 66
Augustine, 49

Bacon, Francis, 19
Badon, Dr., 27
Bancroft, George, 35, 40
Bankruptcy 1995, 87
Bardesanes, 49
Barton, David, 60
Bastiat, Frederic, 82, 83, 93-94, 96
Bible, 18, 56
Bill of Rights, 31
Blackstone, William, 6, 7
Blavatsky, Helena Petrovna, 52-53
Bloom, Allan, 62
Bogomil Heresy, 50
Boston Port Bill, 38
Boston Tea Party, 38
Brewster, William, 24
Brown University, 62
Browne, Robert, 23
Bubonic Plague, 118
Buddhism, 48
Burke, Edmund, 132

Caesar, 16, 77-78
Calvin, John, 19, 21
capitalism, 99
Cathars, 49-50
Catherine of Aragon, 22
charity, 85-86
Charles I, 22, 26

169

Chernobyl, 138-139
Christ, 10, 11, 16-20, 58, 75-76
Christians, 74, 117
Church, Benjamin, 37
churches, 17
Cicero, 6, 113
citizenship, 74-81
civil law, 2
Clark, Fred G., 107
Closing of the American Mind, The, 62
collectivism, 99
college education, 95
Columbus, Christopher, 19
communism, 85, 99, 112
Communist Manifesto, 50, 104
computers, 5-6
Constantine, 17
Constitution of the United States, 38-42, 58, 115
Continental Congress, 38
Copernicus, Nicholaus, 19
Cornwallis, General, 40
Covenanters, 25-26
Cramer, Bishop, 22
criminal justice system, 1
Cromwell, Thomas, 21
Cush, 147

da Vinci, Leonardo, 19
Dale, Sir Thomas, 103
Darrow, Clarence, 66
Darwin, Charles, 51-52, 134
Darwin, Robert, 51
Darwinism, 51
Das Kapital, 51
David, 13
de Montalembert, Mr., 93
de Tocqueville, Alexis, 62, 149-150
de Vattel, Emerich, 37
Debs, Eugene V., 66

Declaration of Independence, 31, 39-40
"Declaration of the Causes and Necessity of Taking Up Arms, The," 39
democracy, 20, 24, 25
Descartes, Rene, 44
Descent of Man, 51-52
Dewey, John, 67, 68
Dickinson, John, 37
"Diggers, the," 112
divorce, 124-125, 126
dust bowl, 133

Earl of Argyll, 25
economics, 99-111
education, 56-73
Edward VI, 22
Elizabeth I, 22, 23
energy taxes, 96-97
Enoch, 10
environmentalism, 133-140
equality, 112-117
Esau, 147
Essay on Human Understanding, 30
ethics, 56-57
Eve, 12

Fabian Socialism, 52
Fabian Societies, 66
Fair Labor Standards Act, 105
families, 12-15, 126-127
"Farmer's Letters to the Inhabitants of the British Colonies," 37
farming, 110-111
Figgie, Harry E., Jr., 87
First Amendment, 58, 75, 116
Fiske, John, 37
flood, the, 46
Franklin, Benjamin, 40-42

170

free enterprise, 134
free will, 7
Fundamental Constitutions for the Government of Carolina, 28

Gage, Thomas, 38
Georgetown University, 116-117
gnosticism, 17, 43-44, 45, 46-50, 52, 53-55
Goethe, 54
Golden Dawn, 52
government, 1, 82-89, 149
Great Society, 35
greenhouse effect, 136-137
Guizot, Francois, 3

Haeckel, Ernst, 53
Hamilton, Patrick, 22
Harris, Benjamin, 60
Hawley Smoot Tariff Bill, 105
Henry VIII, 21, 22
Hereford, Nicholas, 18
Hezekiah, 14
Higginson, Thomas Wentworth, 66
Hinduism, 46, 48
History of Plymouth Plantation, 103
History of the Puritans, 18
Hitler, Adolph, 53-54, 69, 78, 87, 125
Holy Grail, 54
Hooker, Thomas, 25, 26-27, 30-31
Hoover, Herbert, 104-105
How We Live: A Simple Dissection of the Economic Body, 107
Humanist Manifesto, 68
Hutchinson, Governor, 37
Huxley, Julian, 51
Hyperboreh, 53

Intercollegiate Socialist Society (ISS), 66-67, 68
intolerable acts, 34-35

Isaac, 10, 147
Isaiah, 13-14
Isis Unveiled, 53

Jacob, 10, 12
James II, 22, 30
Jamestown Colony, 32, 103
Jefferson, Thomas, 61
Jesus Christ, *see* Christ
Job, 79
John, the Apostle, 6
Josephus, 14

karma, 46
Keating, Charles, 69
Kepler, Johannes, 19
Kettlewell, H. B. D., 51
"Killing Times, the," 26
Knox, John, 19, 22
Kuan, Kuan Chung, 66

Latimer, Bishop, 22
Law, The, 82, 93
League for Industrial Democracy, 66-67, 68
Lemuria, 53
Leslie, Alexander, 25
Letter Concerning Toleration, The, 28, 30
"Levellers, the," 112
Lincoln, Abraham, 69
Lippman, Walter, 66
Litchfield Law School, 63
Locke, John, 3, 24, 25, 27-31, 37, 63-64, 92, 112-113, 115-116
London, Jack, 66
Lowell, James Russell, 3
Lucifer, 53
Luther, Martin, 19, 21

Machiavelli, Niccolo, 19
MacKenzie, George, 26

171

MacMillan, Harold, 104
Madison, James, 91
Mani, 49
Manichaeism, 49, 54
Mann, Horace, 62-63, 69
Marcionism, 49
marriage, 118-127
Marx, Karl, 50-51, 53, 93, 112, 125
Mary of Scotland, 22
Mary Tudor, 22
Mayflower Compact, 24
Mayflower, 24
meekness, 78
Mein Kampf, 87
Methvin, Eugene H., 58
Michelangelo, 19
Milken, Michael, 69
minimum wage, 105, 106
Minor v. Board of Education of Cincinnati, 71
money, 79-81
moral relativism, 121
Moral and Intellectual Inequality of the Races, 53
Mosaic Law, 11, 76, 145
Moses, 10, 12
Mount St. Helens, 137

national debt, 89
National Church of England, 21
National Fast Day, 69
National Industrial Recovery Act, 105
National Recovery Administration, 105
natural law, 2, 5-11, 12-15
Nazis, 125
Neal, Daniel, 18
Nebuchadnezzar, 143-144
Neill, Richard, 153-154
New Age, 47, 54
New Deal, 35, 105, 106

New England Primer, The, 60
Newton, Isaac, 19
Nietzsche, Friedrich, 44
Nimrod, 147
nirvana, 46
Noah, 10, 46, 142, 146

Occult and the Third Reich, The, 54
Of Paternal Power, 29
Of Political or Civil Society, 29-30
Of Property, 29
Of the Dissolution of Government, 30
Of the Extent of the Legislative Power, 30
Of the State of Nature, 28-29
Of the State of War, 29
Old Testament, 1
Origin of Species, 51
Ostara, 54
Otis, James, 35-36

paganism, 48, 148
pantheism, 47, 48
parenting, 59-60, 61
Parsifal, 54
Passel, Peter, 106
Paul the Apostle, 10, 14, 16, 17, 49, 77
Paulicians, 50
Penn, William, 30
Peter, 17, 49
Philip II, 22
Pilgrim Church, 24
pilgrims, 23-25
Plato, 5, 7, 9, 10, 125
Plymouth colony, 32, 103
Plymouth Rock, 24
polio, 118
political correctness, 149
Political Action Committees (PACs), 90-91, 92

Politics, 10, 12-13
printing press, 19
private property, 134
Progressive Education Association, 67
property, 91
Puritans, 21-31, 112
Purvey, John, 18
Pythagoras, 48

Quest for Certainty, 68

Ray, Marcel, 54
Reader's Digest, 58
reason, 7, 8, 44
Reasonableness of Christianity, The, 3, 30
Reformation, 18, 19, 20, 21
Renaissance, 19, 20
Republic, The, 125
Reuther, Walter, 66
Ridley, Bishop, 22
Rights of the British Colonies Asserted and Proved, The, 35-36
Rimanoczy, Richard S., 107
Roman Empire, 17, 77-78
Roosevelt, Franklin D., 87, 105

Sartre, Jean-Paul, 44
Saul, 13
secular humanism, 54, 68-69
sexual revolution, 119-120
Shafer, Ron, 64-65
Shaw, George Bernard, 66
Sinclair, Upton, 66
situation ethics, 69
slavery, 115
smallpox, 118
Snow, John Howland, 66
Social Security Act, 105, 106
socialism, 51, 66-68, 82, 93-98, 99-111

Solomon, 13, 79
special interests, 90-92
spiritual law, 2
spotted owl, 135
Stalin, Joseph, 69
Stamp Act, 36
Star Wars, 46
Stokes, J. G. Phelps, 66
Supreme Court, 59, 69-73

Taft, Alphonso, 71
taxation, 32-36, 93-98
Ten Commandments, 57, 69, 75-76
"Ten Pillars of Economic Wisdom," 96, 107-111
Theosophical Society, 52
Thule Society, 53
Tower of Babel, 46
Townshend Act, 36
trade, 1
Treatise Concerning Civil Government, 112
Treatises on Civil Government, The, 28
Treaty of Versailles, 87
Turning of the Tides, The, 66
Tyndale, William, 19
typhoid fever, 118

Uniformity Act, 22
unions, 106
unknown God, 10

Vine, W. E., 25
Voice of Silence, The, 53
von Liebenfels, Jorg Lanz, 54
von Sebottendorf, Baron, 53
voting, 75

Wagner, Richard, 54
Warren, Joseph, 37
Washington, George, 3, 39, 40

Wayne Act, 105
Wells, H. G., 66
Wilkinson, Ellen, 66
Willison, George, 21, 22
Wishart, George, 22
Wittenberg Cathedral, 21
Wycliffe, John, 18, 19

Xenophon, 14

Yamamoto, Admiral, 4

Zorach v. Clauson, 70
Zwengli, Ulrich, 19, 20

About the Author

Born and raised in Fort Worth, Texas, Pauline Cusack graduated from the Arts Educational in London, England. She is a graduate of Stephens College and attended Texas Christian University. After marrying, she lived in Switzerland, where her husband, Michael, was an assistant stage director with the Zurich Opera. They have three sons and three grandsons.

After returning to the United States, she was volunteer precinct worker for Senator Barry Goldwater's campaign and volunteered in the Harris County GOP doing staff work. In 1967 she became the Harris County volunteer chairman, in 1968–69 served as special-events chairman, and in 1970 and and 1972 served in the same capacity for Representative Bill Archer's first congressional campaign.

She was heavily involved in fund-raising in Houston with the Houston Grand Opera as first vice-president and co-chairman of fund-raising. Other local volunteer work included the Houston Heritage Society and the Pin Oak Horse Show. Pauline did several books for "Taping for the Blind," including *A Night to Remember* and *The Penkovsky Papers*.

As a teacher for twenty-three years, she was head of drama and debate at St. Thomas' Episcopal School, producing more than forty-three plays, half of which were Shakespearean dramas. Additionally, she served as faculty sponsor/teacher of the free-market curriculum, the "Ten Pillars of Economic Wisdom." She also taught Sunday school for many years.

After moving to Fredricksburg, Texas, Pauline joined the Gillespie County Republican Women. She was chairman of the Texas Federation of Republican Women's "No Child Left Behind" Education Summit, Austin, Texas. She is immediate past vice president for finance and currently serves as vice president for legislation of the Texas Federation of Republican Women. Pauline is chairman of the board of trustees for the TFRW Education Foundation. Pauline travels around the state speaking to clubs and organizations about policy and political issues. She works on state and local fund-raising, promoting Republican and conservative causes and candidates.